Foundations *to* Political Science:

The Study Guide 2021

R. L. COHEN

Humanities
ACADEMIC PUBLISHERS

ISBN: 978-1-988557-04-5

Published Location: Published in New Zealand

Imprint Company Name for Publication: Humanities Academic Publishers

A catalogue record for this book is available from the National Library of New Zealand.

Kei te pātengi raraunga o Te Puna Mātauranga o Aotearoa te whakarārangi o tēnei pukapuka.

Contents

CHAPTER 1

Key definition in Political Science

1. In a republic, who is in charge?

   a. the people

   b. the president

   c. the Supreme Court

   d. the bureaucracy

2. What does the theory of pluralism mean?

   a. Pluralism is the ideal of multicultural coexistence.

   b. Pluralism suggests that people can influence government through the many interest groups that spring up to champion everything from fighting for energy independence to banning abortions.

   c. Pluralism suggests that people can influence politicians by advocating their views on a large scale.

   d. Pluralism is the idea that one can believe in both Christian and Muslim religious tenets.

3. According to the pluralist theory, where is influence displayed in government?

   a. religious groups

   b. interest groups

    c. political groups

    d. union

4. Where does the elite theory place the source of political influence?

    a. "power elite" in government, the judicial branch, and the military

    b. "power elite" in college institutions, business, and the Central Intelligence Agency

    c. "power elite" in unions, corporations, and banks

    d. "power elite" in government, corporations, and the military

5. Where does the elite theory place political power?

    a. status based on economic influence and religious background

    b. status based on economic influence and leadership position

    c. status based on economic influence and academic background

    d. status based on economic influence and party affiliation

6. What does the social movement theory identify as the source of influence?

    a. controversial uprisings/movements

    b. religious uprisings/movements

    c. popular uprisings/movements

    d. economic uprisings/movements

7. Where does the social movement theory locate political power?

    a. strength of mass demands

    b. strength of student demands

    c. strength of union demands

    d. strength of private demands

8. What is a republic?

   a. A government system that rests ultimate governing power in its people, who may rule directly or via representatives.

   b. A government system that rests most governing power in the elite selected for authority based on obtaining superior education.

   c. A government system that rests none of the governing power in its people but instead allows a single individual to exercise sole political control to ensure the well-being of all people.

   d. All of the above.

9. The principle of checks and balances ensures that which branch of government has the authority to block the other branches?

   a. the executive branch

   b. the judicial branch

   c. the legislative branch

   d. all three branches

10. The Declaration of Independence explained the role of government—securing each individual's three rights. Which of the following is one of those rights?

    a. life

    b. freedom

    c. success

    d. none of the above

11. The Declaration of Independence explained the role of government—securing each individual's three rights. Which of the following is one of those rights?

    a. wealth

    b. land

    c. liberty

    d. none of the above

12. Which of the following is not one of the seven big ideas espoused in the Declaration of Independence?

    a. liberty

    b. individualism

    c. freedom of religion

    d. freedom to bear arms

13. What is the definition of freedom?

    a. It means that the government will protect one's life, one's liberty, and one's property from the coercion of others (excluding government) in order to permit you to pursue the goals you define for yourself.

    b. It means that the government will protect one's life, one's liberty, and one's property from the coercion of others (including the government) in order to permit you to pursue the goals you define for yourself.

    c. It means that the government will protect one's life, one's liberty, and one's guns from the coercion of others (including the government) in order to permit you to pursue the goals you define for yourself.

    d. none of the above

14. What is the view of negative liberty?

    a. Freedom is granted with limited restrictions.

    b. Freedom is the absence of constraints.

    c. Freedom is the inclusion of constraints.

    d. None of the above.

15. What is the definition of positive liberty?

    a. The freedom to pursue one's goals with government restrictions.

    b. The freedom to pursue one's goals with some exceptions.

    c. The freedom to pursue one's goals.

    d. The freedom to pursue one's goals without government control.

16. What is the concept of individualism?

    a. The idea that individuals, with some government assistance, are responsible for their own well-being.

    b. The notion that individuals, with some assistance from the greater society, are responsible for their own well-being.

    c. The idea that individuals, not the society or the community, or the government, are responsible for their own well-being.

    d. None of the above.

17. What do social democrats believe?

    a. Members of a society are responsible for one another except for some assistance from the government.

    b. Members of a society are responsible for one another and should support other developing countries.

    c. Members of a society are responsible for one another.

    d. None of the above

18. Social democracies are based on _____, the idea that people have a tight bond and are responsible for one another.

    a. solidarity

    b. social cohesiveness

    c. interdependence

    d. social collaboration

19. Which economist famously wrote, "The world runs on individuals pursuing their separate interests"?

    a. Susan Richards

    b. Michael Samuels

    c. Milton Friedman

    d. Roger Hernandez

20. Which sociologist defined the State as a "human community that (successfully) claims the monopoly of the legitimate use of physical force within a given territory"?

    a. Milton Friedman

    b. Max Weber

    c. Karl Marx

    d. Juan Domingo Perón

21. True or False: democracy's etymology comes from the Greek word demos ("the people") and kratos (power).

22. Which politician said that, in a totalitarian state, there is "all within the state, none outside the state and none against the state"?

    a. Benito Musolini

    b. Donald Trump

    c. Adolf Hitler

    d. Iosif Stalin

23. Which is the last totalitarian regime left in the world?

    a. China

    b. Russia

    c. Cuba

    d. North Korea

24. True or False: Pluralism developed after the end of the First World War and reached its height during the 1950s and 1960s.

25. True or False: Positive liberty is based on the claim that "I am free to the extent that I achieve self-mastery."

Discussion questions

1. Define contemporary American culture.

2. Identify current theocratic, authoritarian, and totalitarian regimes throughout the world. What are the threats these regimes pose to American democratic leadership?

3. What does the Manifest Destiny represent in American political culture?

4. Define fascism. What are the contemporary forms of fascism?

5. True or False. America is a democracy. Why? Why not?

6. True or False: Russia is a democracy. Why? Why not?

7. What do social democrats believe in?

Video Resources

USA.gov Channel https://www.youtube.com/usagov1

Icount https://icount.com/

PBS Frontline http://www.pbs.org/wgbh/pages/frontline/watch/

Firing Line Debates https://www.hoover.org/library-archives/collections/firing-line

Bill Moyers http://billmoyers.com/

President Benjamin Harrison (1889-1893) https://youtu.be/pU4gGEL5c8g

Oldest Footage of a President https://youtu.be/gAesU_GOe_4

Introduction to Political Science https://www.youtube.com/watch?v=Xhjl-MvnqAc

Website Resources

Data and Statistics about the United States https://www.usa.gov/statistics

A Chronology of US Historical Documents www.ushistory.org/documents/

The Founders' Constitution http://press-pubs.uchicago.edu/founders/

Follow the Money http://www.followthemoney.org/

Political Resource Directory http://politicalresources.com/

The Internet Classics Archive classics.mit.edu

The Online Library of Liberty http://oll.libertyfund.org/

CHAPTER 2

American Political Culture

1. True or False: The American founders based their ideas for a new form of government on the philosophies of John Locke.

2. Americans largely accepted the political ideas of which philosopher, whose ideas of political change challenged British ideology?

   a. Thomas Hobbes

   b. Patrick Henry

   c. John Calvin

   d. John Locke

3. Why did the colonists find the philosophical work of John Locke the most appealing?

   a. It laid the groundwork for a completely anarchical society, which is what the founding fathers ultimately wanted.

   b. It introduced the idea that a social contract was conditional on the protection of rights and could be revoked if the government failed to protect those rights.

   c. It upheld the morality of slavery as a necessary evil to successful economics in a country that would struggle otherwise.

   d. Another country had previously based their structure of government on his ideas and it worked out well for them.

4. Under a _____ government, a small group of elites exercise unlimited power over individuals in all aspects of life.

   a. totalitarian

   b. theocratic --- Consider This: A theocracy refers to government rule by a religious order.

   c. authoritarian

   d. republican

5. Why do many Americans believe that they have limited power to change the course of government?

   a. Government is viewed as distant and remote.

   b. Their votes are counted the same as everyone else's.

   c. Government exists to oppose the elite.

   d. Few people try to contact their representatives. --- Consider This: Federal elected officials receive messages from hundreds of constituents daily.

6. Which of the following statements expresses the central idea of democracy?

   a. Every person in the country should be allowed to vote. --- Consider This: Voting is not the defining feature of democracy; elections take place in dictatorships, but they are not considered free.

   b. Ordinary people want to rule themselves and are capable of doing so.

   c. Security, along with religious laws and values, is the most important function of government.

   d. Governing should be carried out by a single, enlightened leader.

7. An important aspect of representative democracy is _____.

   a. a class structure that lets the elite rise to the top

    b. periodic elections so citizens can replace those whose views no longer reflect the views of the majority

    c. elections that limit competition so that citizens aren't confused by too many choices --- Consider This: This form of election for this purpose is not consistent with the free and fair elections characteristic of representative democracy.

    d. control over a candidate's message so that he or she doesn't mislead the people

8. True or False: American Civil War is arguably the darkest and bloodiest hour in America's history.

9. True or False: British political culture embraces community and communitarianism, insisting that people be protected by the government.

10. True or False: American political culture provides a belief in core values of equality, socialism, and popular democracy.

11. How do Americans understand freedom?

    a. Freedom from the government

    b. Freedom to do whatever they want to do

    c. Freedom to make political choices

    4. Economic freedom

12. True or False: Individualism has an emphasis on the collective whole rather than individual rights

13. What does equality mean in the American political system?

    a. All people within a specific society have the equal rights, liberties, and status

    b. Equality of opportunity.

c. Equality under the law.

d. None of the above.

14. Democracy is a decision-making process by which:

    a. Autocrats decide what policies are the best for the country.

    b. groups register their preferences for their officials and the policies they promise.

    c. individuals register their preferences for their officials and the policies they promise.

    d. None of the above.

15. Is the United States considered a democracy?

    a. Yes. Absolutely.

    b. America is both a democracy and a republic. A representative democracy, to be more precise.

    c. No.

    d. None of the above.

16. Which is the initiative that allows the citizens citizens to have direct access to creating a democratic state

    a. A referendum

    b. A plebiscite

    c. Advertising campaigns

    d. Rioting

17. What is a good example of the referendum as a way of direct democracy?

    a. Proposition 18, 2018.

    b. Proposition 5, 2001.

    c. Proposition 13, 2012.

    d. Proposition 17, 2020.

18. What do Americans understand by equal opportunity?

a. the idea that first class citizens are the ones that should influence politics and achieve economic success.

b. the idea that every American has the same chance to influence politics and achieve economic success regardless of their race, gender, or class.

c. the idea that every white American has the same chance to influence politics and achieve economic success regardless of their race, gender, or class.

d. the idea that Americans have the chance to influence politics and achieve economic success according to each one's contribution.

19. True or False: Ideologies are the competing narratives we create to explain disagreements

20. True or False: In the American political spectrum, conservatives on the right call for more regulation of the economy.

21. American conservatives do not believe in:

a. reduced government spending

b. liberal and unorthodox moral values

c. personal responsibility

d. robust national defense

22. True or False: In the American political spectrum, liberals on the left call for more government regulation, in broad and diverse areas such as social welfare programs, universal health care, and free preschool programs.

23. Which of the following is incorrect?

a. Modern liberals in America value cultural diversity.

b. Modern liberals in America call for public intervention in the economy.

    c. Modern liberals in America value individual's rights to a lifestyle based on their own social and moral positions.

    d. Modern liberals in America demand mandatory religious education.

24. True or False: Modern liberals strictly adhere to Locke's classical emphasis on abundant liberty.

25. Why are social issues a source of division between conservatives and liberals?

    a. Conservatives and liberals cannot understand each other

    b. There is no middle point between both groups

    c. Social conservatives put a priority on the government preserving a traditional social order

    d. None of the above

Discussion Questions

1. According to the text, what is political culture?

2. What is the concept of limited government?

3. What is the concept of liberalism?

4. True or False: American political culture focuses on individualism more than collectivism.

5. True or False: Americans understand freedom as freedom from government. Equality in America is equality under the law.

6. What are the values and cultural beliefs that are most ingrained in American citizens?

Video resources

USA.gov Channel https://www.youtube.com/usagov1

Icount https://icount.com/

American political culture - Harvard University https://www.youtube.com/watch?v=kUXCGYCJiZE

Political Culture - Harvard University - Thomas Patterson https://edx-video.net/d1c70b49-878a-45ad-9a37-7a071b93a1a5-mp4_720p.mp4

Civics and Government https://www.pbslearningmedia.org/subjects/social-studies/civics-and-government/

Website resources

US History - American Political Culture https://www.ushistory.org/gov/4a.asp

American political culture - University of Minnesota http://open.lib.umn.edu/americangovernment/chapter/6-1-political-culture/

The Alexis de Tocqueville Tour: Exploring Democracy in America https://www.c-span.org/series/?tocqueville

Smithsonian: History and Culture http://www.si.edu/history_and_culture

Data and Statistics about the United States https://www.usa.gov/statistics/

A Chronology of US Historical Documents www.ushistory.org/documents/

CHAPTER 3

Politics and Economic Models

1. Rules are used to _____.

    a. decide who gets power and influence

    b. decide who gets material resources and how

    c. govern the country

    d. determine who will win or lose future power struggles

2. The market controls economic decisions in a(n) _____ economy.

    a. socialist

    b. capitalist

    c. authoritarian

    d. totalitarian

3. In the United States, businesses have substantial freedom from government interference, but the government will step in and regulate the economy from time to time to guarantee individual rights. The United States uses which type of economic system?

    a. socialism

    b. laissez-faire capitalism

    c. communism

    d. regulated capitalism

4. In socialist economies, control over economic decisions is exercised by _____.

    a. the market

    b. the government

    c. supply and demand forces

    d. a vote by the people

5. A capitalist economy is an economic system that relies on the _____ to determine who should have material goods.

    a. government

    b. people

    c. top businesses

    d. market

6. Some countries in Western Europe utilize a hybrid system that gives individuals more control over their personal lives and a government that supports equality, which is a form of _____.

    a. capitalist democracy

    b. Marxist utopia

    c. totalitarianism

    d. authoritarian capitalism

7. A political system in which the state holds all the power over the social order is known as _____.

    a. a republic

    b. an authoritarian government

    c. a capitalist government

    d. a pure democracy

8. In non-authoritarian systems, _____.

    a. there is no government at all

    b. the government regulates people's behavior but grants considerable freedoms

    c. the government has total control over people's behavior

    d. the government has all the power

9. A _____ government combines an authoritarian government with a socialist economy.

    a. totalitarian

    b. anarchic

    c. democratic

    d. monarchical

10. Which is a characteristic of a democratic government?

    a. The government rules over subjects.

    b. There is usually one central head that is in charge of all laws and regulations.

    c. The government dictates how its people can behave.

    d. The citizens have considerable power to make the rules that govern them.

11. The absence of a government and laws is a characteristic of _____.

    a. totalitarianism

    b. anarchy

    c. authoritarianism

    d. democracy

12. A person who believes that there should be no government or laws whatsoever is most likely a(n) _____.

    a. communist

    b. socialist

    c. capitalist

    d. anarchist

13. The principle that serves as the basis for democracy and allows people to have a hand in the rules that govern them is known as _____.

    a. authoritarianism

    b. socialism

    c. popular sovereignty

    d. totalitarianism

14. Individuals who must submit to a government authority under which they have no rights are _____.

    a. elitists

    b. citizens

    c. democrats

    d. subjects

15. True or False: Rules are directives that determine how resources are allocated, and they determine how we try to get the things we want.

16. True or False: In a socialist economy, the market controls economic decisions.

17. True or False: In a laissez-faire capitalist society, there are no restrictions on the market at all, making the economy subject to wild swings up and down.

18. True or False: Politics is the system or organization for exercising authority over a body of people.

19. True or False: Those who live under an authoritarian-style government are known as citizens.

20. True or False: A totalitarian government combines an authoritarian government with a socialist economy.

21. True or False: Powerful national government, collectivism, and a belief in social hierarchies are fundamental to American political culture.

22. True or False: An economic conservative would favor lower taxes and limited government regulation of the economy.

23. True or False: Having control over the political narrative does not give anyone an advantage or a disadvantage.

24. True or False: Prices represent the equilibrium point at which the quantity of goods supplied by producers equals the amount required by consumers.

25. True or False: Henri de Saint-Simon was the first to coin the term "socialism" as the alternative system to capitalism who could have granted equal opportunities to the people.

Discussion questions

1. Define capitalism. Identify countries with a capitalist economy. What are the common characteristics these countries share?

2. Define socialism. Identify countries with a socialist economy. What are the common characteristics these countries share?

3. True or False: China has a capitalist economy. Why? Why not?

4. Define state capitalism. Identify countries with a state capitalist economy.

5. Since the dissolution of the Soviet Union, the vast majority of the countries in the world has adopted various forms of capitalism. Why? Explain the reasons.

6. What is a capitalist democracy? Is there a connection between capitalism and democracy?

Video Resources

USA.gov Channel https://www.youtube.com/usagov1

Icount https://icount.com/

PBS Frontline http://www.pbs.org/wgbh/pages/frontline/watch/

TED Talk - Eric X. Li: A Tale of Two Political Systems https://www.ted.com/talks/eric_x_li_a_tale_of_two_political_systems

The Collision of Capitalism and Democracy https://sc4.idm.oclc.org/login?url=https://sc4.idm.oclc.org/login?url=http://digital.films.com/PortalPlaylists.aspx?wID=97865&xtid=70940

Heaven on Earth: The Rise and Fall of Socialism Series https://sc4.idm.oclc.org/login?url=https://sc4.idm.oclc.org/login?url=http://digital.films.com/PortalPlaylists.aspx?seriesID=12584&wID=97865

Marx Reloaded https://sc4.idm.oclc.org/login?url=https://sc4.idm.oclc.org/login?url=http://digital.films.com/PortalPlaylists.aspx?wID=97865&xtid=52228

Website resources

20th century US Capitalism and Regulation (Khan Academy) https://www.khanacademy.org/humanities/us-history/history-survey/

us-history-survey/v/20th-century-capitalism-and-regulation-in-the-united-states

Communism: Karl Marx to Joseph Stalin https://europe.unc.edu/iron-curtain/history/communism-karl-marx-to-joseph-stalin/

American Socialists www.americansocialists.org

Data and Statistics about the United States https://www.usa.gov/statistics

A Chronology of US Historical Documents www.ushistory.org/documents/

Follow the Money http://www.followthemoney.org/

Political Resource Directory http://politicalresources.com/

The Internet Classics Archive classics.mit.edu

The Online Library of Liberty http://oll.libertyfund.org/

CHAPTER 4

Federalism

1. The complex interplay between state, local, and national governments stretches all the way back to the debates between:

   a. Federalists and Whigs.

   b. Federalists and Anti-Federalists.

   c. Republicans and Democrats.

   d. Anti-Federalists and Whigs.

2. Which form of government favors a central government exercising all or most political authority?

   a. unitary

   b. confederation

   c. loosely coupled federation

   d. federal

3. When the federal power is weak, providing defense and economic benefits, one can consider it an

   a. confederation

   b. federation

   c. republic

   d. democracy

4. Which level(s) of government is/are responsible for regulating business?

   a. federal

   b. state

   c. local

   d. federal and state

5. The hybrid developed by the delegates at the Constitutional Convention was a _____ system.

   a. confederal

   b. federal

   c. unitary

   d. socialist

6. Which of the following is not a weakness of a confederation?

   a. more local control over policy

   b. weak central authority

   c. a variety of contradictory state actions

   d. unclear individual rights

7. Public education would be a good example of what kind of power or powers?

   a. federal

   b. state

   c. concurrent

   d. local

8. Which of the following is not an advantage of federalism?

   a. coordination across levels of government

   b. protecting individual rights

c. providing sources of innovation

d. responsiveness to local needs

9. Which of the following is not a disadvantage of federalism?

a. coordination

b. individual rights

c. poor policies

d. inequalities across layers

10. Which of the following is not a granted power to Congress?

a. organizing state elections

b. handling US foreign policy

c. establishing post offices

d. raising an army

11. What is the name for a power that is explicitly found in the United States Constitution?

a. enumerated

b. necessary and proper

c. implied

d. informal

12. powers could be thought of as those implied by but not explicitly named in the Constitution.

a. Inherent

b. Enumerated

c. Expressed

d. Concurrent

13. Which amendment to the Constitution provides the foundation for states' rights?

    a. Fourth

    b. Tenth

    c. Twelfth

    d. Fourteenth

14. The Tenth Amendment is most likely favored by

    a. big-government advocates.

    b. those favoring dual federalism.

    c. small-government advocates.

    d. those with a strong liberal ideology.

15. The Tenth Amendment relates to and demonstrates best which type of powers?

    a. reserved

    b. concurrent

    c. inherent

    d. implied

16. Which of the following is not an example of a reserved power?

    a. organizing state elections

    b. coining money

    c. public education

    d. public health

17. Being able to use one's driver's license in any state is an example of the _____ clause.

    a. necessary and proper

    b. full faith and credit

c. supremacy

d. inherent powers

18. Which clause of the Constitution says that each state should recognize and uphold laws passed by any other state?

a. necessary and proper

b. full faith and credit

c. supremacy

d. inherent powers

19. Building railways, borrowing money, and regulating business are examples of : powers.

a. police

b. reserved

c. inherent

d. concurrent

20. federalism argues for the clear division of governing authority between national and state governments.

a. Dual

b. Cooperative

c. Coaptive

d. New

21. If Virginia law conflicts with federal law, which clause argues for federal law to be superior?

a. supremacy

b. full faith and credit

c. elasticity

d. inherent powers

22. The clause says that the national government may wield powers "necessary and proper" to support its function.

 a. supremacy

 b. full faith and credit

 c. elasticity

 d. inherent powers

23. Which of the following is not an example of a concurrent power?

 a. education

 b. transportation

 c. taxation

 d. national defense

24. Block grants provide funds for

 a. elections

 b. any use

 c. specific use

 d. urban growth

25. Which of the following is a key feature of New Federalism?

 a. grants in aid

 b. heavy use of block grants

 c. limited state income tax

 d. increased income tax

26. is defined as the transfer of authority from national to state or local governments.

 a. Supremacy

 b. Devolution

c. Elastic

d. Power-seeking theory

27. Who are more likely to prefer state control of an issue?

a. Republicans

b. Democrats

c. Socialists

d. Communists

28. The states and federal government are _____ in progressive federalism.

a. partners

b. competitors

c. separate

d. alienated

29. Through the Court's interpretation of the necessary and proper clause, which institution of government is most affected?

a. the presidency

b. Congress

c. the bureaucracy

d. independent commissions

30. Which Supreme Court case extended to individuals the right to challenge federal statutes on the grounds that they interfere with powers reserved to the states?

a. Medellin v. Texas

b. Citizens United v. Clinton

c. Gonzales v. Oregon

d. Bond v. United States

31. Feelings of nationalism help maintain the federal balance by instilling loyalty to which level(s) of government?

    a. federal

    b. state

    c. local

    d. all of the above

32. The Supreme Court's review of a law passed by Congress best demonstrates which American government principle related to federalism?

    a. checks and balances

    b. supremacy clause

    c. nationalism

    d. unfunded mandates

33. Federalism operates along a _____ dimension.

    a. vertical

    b. horizontal

    c. lateral

    d. multidimensional

34. Which group best demonstrates civic voluntarism?

    a. members of Congress

    b. local school board members

    c. district court judges

    d. local police officers

35. What two layers of government interacted to define dual federalism?

    a. national and state

    b. state and local

c. national and local

d. national and the nonprofit sector

36. Which "cake" metaphor was introduced during the New Deal?

a. layer cake

b. Bundt cake

c. marble cake

d. none of the above

37. A large, diverse and fragmented nation can be bound together through

a. nationalism

b. federalism

c. voting

d. borders

38. A reason for historical shifts in the Supreme Court can be traced to

a. state courts

b. the bureaucracy

c. the party in power

d. the president

39. Federalism is the relationship between different levels of

a. government

b. people

c. bureaucracies

d. states

40. Powers necessary for the president to fulfill their duties but not named in the Constitution are known as _____ powers.

    a. inherent

    b. concurrent

    c. diffused

    d. mixed

41. Congress's authority to establish a national bank exemplifies its _____ powers.

    a. concurrent

    b. inherent

    c. reserved

    d. granted

42. The "and proper clause" provides Congress's power over issues not explicitly found in the Constitution.

    a. necessary

    b. useful

    c. immediate

    d. utilized

Discussion Questions

1. Does federalism result in greater competition between state and local governments? Why, and in what areas might it?

2. What is the foundation for states' rights?

3. In what policy areas is there a clear distinction for national responsibility? Are there any recent actions by political officials that may refute this?

4. Why are the courts necessary in discussing federalism?

5. Discuss the question of concurrent powers.

6. Discuss the advantages and disadvantages of federalism.

Video Resources

Federalism in Education Made Simple http://www.youtube.com/watch?v=Ebf1HLiZeyY

Federalism in the United States - Khan Academy https://www.khanacademy.org/humanities/us-government-and-civics/us-gov-foundations/us-gov-relationship-between-the-states-and-the-federal-government/v/federalism-in-the-united-states

Federalism - Bill of Rights Institute https://billofrightsinstitute.org/videos/federalism-homework-help

Federalism in the United States - C Span Classroom www.c-span.org/classroom/document/?7105

Chief Justice Roberts on the Role of the Supreme Court http://www.cspanclassroom.org/Topics/FE/Federalism.aspx

The Rise of Nationalism in 2017 https://www.youtube.com/watch?v=cH3I8nFyp6g

Website Resources

James Madison's Federalist no. 10 and the American Political System http://cstl-cla.semo.edu/renka/renka_papers/madison.htm

Timeline of Federalism in the United States http://www.education.ne.gov/SS/CSSAP%20Modules/CSSAP%20First%20Phase%20Modules/federalism/timeline.html

Understanding   Federalism   https://www.archives.gov/legislative/ resources/education/federalism

Federalism - Political Science - Research Guides at University of British Columbia http://guides.library.ubc.ca/politicalscience/federalism

Cornell University Law School Legal Information Institute http://www. law.cornell.edu/wex/federalism

The definition of a nationalist https://www.cnn.com/2018/10/23/politics/nationalism-explainer-trnd/index.html

Nationalism Has Gotten a Bad Reputation. But It's What America Needs Right Now http://time.com/5431089/trump-white-nationalism-bible/

CHAPTER 5

Declaration of Independence and Constitution

1. The document America considers its "owners' manual" is

   a. the Declaration of Independence.

   b. the Articles of Confederation.

   c. the Constitution.

   d. the Magna Carta.

2. The document that takes the ideas of the Declaration of Independence and turns them into laws and institutions is

   a. the Articles of Confederation.

   b. the Magna Carta.

   c. the Mayflower Compact.

   d. the Constitution.

3. There are _____ articles in the United States Constitution and _____ amendments in the Bill of Rights.

   a. 7, 10

   b. 7, 27

   c. 10, 17

   d. 7, 26

4. Article 7 requires _____ states to ratify the Constitution of 1787.

   a. all

   b. thirteen

   c. six

   d. nine

5. All of the following are features that propelled the framers toward the Constitutional Convention of 1787, except

   a. representation.

   b. violent borders.

   c. social mobility.

   d. abolitionism.

6. In England, in the eighteenth century, the notion that members of Parliament should be guided by their sense of "the general good" regardless of the district they represented was known as

   a. constituency service.

   b. trustee representation.

   c. delegate representation.

   d. "better men" representation.

7. One Act of Parliament the colonists found particularly repugnant required them to house British troops in barns and warehouses; it was called the

   a. Stamp Act.

   b. Redcoat Accommodation Act.

   c. Quartering Act.

   d. English Occupation Act.

8. The Boston Massacre was precipitated by the

    a. Impoundment Act.

    b. Tea Party.

    c. Townshend Act.

    d. Amistad.

9. Due to continued requirements for the colonists to house, or "quarter," British soldiers at colonists' expense wrote into the Bill of Rights

    a. the Fifth Amendment.

    b. the Fourth Amendment.

    c. the Third Amendment.

    d. the Second Amendment.

10. The key statement of American political philosophy is

    a. the Constitution.

    b. the Emancipation Proclamation.

    c. the Mayflower Compact.

    d. the Declaration of Independence.

11. The colonists favored the representation model where the legislature members responded to constituents' desires, known as

    a. the trustee model.

    b. the parliamentary model.

    c. the delegate model.

    d. the politico model.

12. The Declaration of Independence was adopted on

    a. July 4, 1774.

    b. July 4, 1775.

    c. July 4, 1776.

    d. July 4, 1787.

13. The Declaration of Independence details all of the following American ideals except

    a. life, liberty, and the pursuit of happiness.

    b. capitalism and the protection of private property.

    c. all men are created equal.

    d. people form governments to protect rights that they are "endowed" with and cannot be taken away.

14. The political philosopher that had an enormous impact on revolutionary America and the framers' thinking was

    a. Tocqueville.

    b. Robespierre.

    c. Hobbes.

    d. Locke.

15. The second half of the Declaration of Independence lists twenty-seven

    a. God-given rights.

    b. principles of government.

    c. grievances against King George III.

    d. principles of democracy.

16. Identify the three complaints against the English Crown that dominate the Declaration of Independence.

    a. representation, occupying army, loss of an independent court

    b. representation, taxes, loss of an independent court

    c. taxation without representation, the tax on tea, and British impressments of American sailors

d. taxation without representation, the quartering of soldiers, and the Stamp Act

17. The Declaration of Independence states that liberty is a right that is

a. quite important.

b. fundamental to happiness.

c. unalienable.

d. subject to the whims of governments—it can be taken away.

18. In 1776, for the first time in world history, the American colonists claimed that government

a. must be limited.

b. must protect private property.

c. derives its power from the consent of the governed.

d. must be subject to frequent elections.

19. The Founding Father who stated: "that laws and institutions must go hand in hand with the progress of the human mind" was

a. George Washington.

b. James Madison.

c. Thomas Jefferson.

d. John Adams.

20. The Articles of Confederation were approved by the First Continental Congress in

a. 1620.

b. 1776.

c. 1777.

d. 1787.

21. Under the Articles of Confederation, ___ votes were required on important matters.

    a. thirteen

    b. seven

    c. four

    d. nine

22. Among the severe obstacles to the new government under the Articles of Confederation,

    a. Congress could not raise taxes and had no money of its own.

    b. Virginia dominated all policy discussions.

    c. The southern states were in open rebellion.

    d. North Carolina had brokered treaties with foreign powers.

23. The provision that all thirteen states must approve any changes to the Articles of Confederation

    a. facilitated the amendment process.

    b. made it difficult to conduct foreign affairs.

    c. gave the states too little power.

    d. made it virtually impossible to amend the Articles.

24. A major lesson learned from our experience under the Articles of Confederation

    a. was that a strong confederation of states was impossible.

    b. was that a weak central government left the nation vulnerable.

    c. was the need for a Supreme Court.

    d. was the alliance between Rhode Island and South Carolina.

25. The constitutional deliberations were

    a. open to the public

b. very quick

c. secret

d. attended by delegates from only eight states

26. The Articles showed the founding fathers that a weak government could

a. support rights

b. fail to protect rights

c. create new rights

d. abuse power

27. The Founders adopted a federal system

a. because they hoped King George III would approve.

b. because they were inspired by John Locke, who advocated such a division of powers.

c. because the division of sovereignty between a strong central government and regional governments is a basic principle of all democratic governments.

d. as a compromise between those who wanted a strong central government and those who wanted to retain strong state governments.

28. Which of the following is not a difference between the Virginia Plan and the New Jersey Plan?

a. The Virginia Plan created stronger state governments.

b. The New Jersey Plan created a single legislature, whereas the Virginia Plan called for a bicameral legislature.

c. The Virginia Plan strengthened the national government, whereas the New Jersey Plan weakened the national government.

d. The New Jersey Plan had multiple chief executives, whereas the Virginia Plan created a one-person executive.

29. The Great, or Connecticut, Compromise

    a. provided strong powers to state governments.

    b. established a legislature with equal state representation in the Senate and proportional representation in the House of Representatives.

    c. limited the importation of slaves until 1808.

    d. created a confederacy of state governments.

30. Some delegates at the Constitutional Convention were concerned that an executive would be

    a. too powerful.

    b. too weak.

    c. too subject to "the whims of the people."

    d. someone who was not an American.

31. The delegates did not want people electing the president because they felt people

    a. would be swayed by political parties

    b. would not vote

    c. had enough information or wisdom

    d. did not want to elect the president

32. Why did the framers not give the popular-vote winner the presidency?

    a. They did not trust the judgment of voters.

    b. Women could not vote.

    c. The country had a bad history of electing corrupt politicians.

    d. The Electoral College was more efficient.

33. The number of electors in a state is based on

    a. the number of people in the state.

    b. the number of voters in the state.

c. the number of senators plus the number of members of the House of Representatives.

d. the number of members in the state legislature.

34. For each power described in the Constitution for a branch of government,

a. there is an appropriation process independent of the other branches.

b. there is "countervailing" power.

c. there is a federal agency.

d. there is a way for the other branches to destroy that branch.

35. The president is the commander in chief, but Congress has the power to declare war. This situation is an example of

a. the imperial presidency.

b. the imperial Congress.

c. checks and balances.

d. judicial neutrality.

36. How did the Founders treat slavery in the Constitution?

a. It was not important.

b. It was very divisive, so they had to tackle it head-on.

c. They were unified in their desire to eliminate it.

d. It was very divisive, so they did not mention it directly.

37. The practice of counting slaves as fractional "persons" for representation in the House of Representatives is known as

a. The "Not-Quite" Compromise.

b. The Three-Fifths Compromise.

c. The Two-Thirds Compromise.

d. The Three-Quarters Compromise.

38. During the Constitutional Convention, the state with the highest percentage of slaves out of the total population, at 43 percent, was

    a. Virginia.

    b. Massachusetts.

    c. Texas.

    d. South Carolina.

39. If the institution of slavery had not been protected in the Constitution,

    a. the southern states would have walked out.

    b. Massachusetts would have immediately abolished slavery.

    c. North Carolina would have seceded from the Union.

    d. Texas would have never been admitted to the Union.

40. The first three words of the Constitution are

    a. "Fourscore and seven . . . "

    b. "In order to . . . "

    c. "We the People . . . "

    d. "My fellow Americans . . . "

41. In 1787, a member of the House of Representatives had around 30,000 constituents. Today that number is approximately

    a. 50,000.

    b. 150,000.

    c. 350,000.

    d. 700,000.

42. A large-scale program like Social Security is constitutionally legitimate because

    a. Congress can write any law it deems "necessary and proper."

    b. there is a need to protect older people.

c. older people vote.

d. the executive branch has extensive powers to make laws under Article 2.

43. Far and away, the most extended and most detailed section of the Constitution is

a. the First Amendment.

b. Article 1.

c. Article 2.

d. Article 3.

44. Constitutionally, members of the US House of Representatives must be_____ years of age.

a. 18

b. 25

c. 30

d. 35

45. Constitutionally, members of the US Senate must be_____ years of age.

a. 18

b. 25

c. 30

d. 35

46. All of the following are powers granted to Congress under article 1, section 8, of the Constitution except

a. the power to declare war.

b. the power to command the armed forces.

c. the power to collect taxes.

d. the power to coin money.

47. The necessary and proper clause

   a. allows Congress to regulate commerce.

   b. allows Congress to control the money supply.

   c. gives Congress a great deal of creative leeway.

   d. it has defined boundaries.

48. According to article 1, section 9 of the Constitution, habeas corpus may not be suspended unless

   a. Americans gather to protest for the overthrow of the government.

   b. an election takes place.

   c. a majority of Congress votes to suspend.

   d. in cases of rebellion or invasion, public safety requires it.

49. Originally, each state decided how it choose its electors for the Electoral College, but now

   a. every state has the minority party select them.

   b. Twenty-seven states have the people make a choice.

   c. Seventeen states have the people make a choice.

   d. all states have the people make a choice.

50. Treaties made by presidents are constitutionally valid if

   a. two-thirds of the Senate approves.

   b. two-thirds of the House of Representatives approve.

   c. three-quarters of the Senate approve.

   d. three-quarters of the House of Representatives approve.

51. The case in which Chief Justice John Marshall established judicial review, giving the Supreme Court the power to overturn Congress's act, was

   a. Wickard v. Filburn.

b. Brown v. Topeka Board of Education.

c. Marbury v. Madison.

d. Barron v. Baltimore.

Discussion Questions

1. What weaknesses were inherent in the Articles of Confederation?

2. How did the ideas that inspired the colonists to rebel shape the Constitution and the Bill of Rights?

3. What were the arguments put forth by the Federalists and the Anti-federalists? Which arguments do you support?

4. How do Americans change the Constitution? Is the Constitution a living document?

5. Discuss the Articles of Confederation, focusing on how the government functioned with a centralized administration. Be sure to highlight how power was distributed then and what it means for current views of states' rights. From our modern viewpoint, why does it seem inevitable that the Articles did not survive? What did the Articles teach us about government?

6. Does democracy work? One way to frame the rest of the course, especially from this text's viewpoint, is to ask the "big" questions and explore them thematically throughout the course using the Constitution as the fulcrum.

Video Resources

The Declaration of Independence - Khan Academy www.khanacademy.org/humanities/us-history/road-to-revolution/the-american-revolution/v/the-declaration-of-independence

The Preamble to the Constitution - Khan Academy www.khanacademy.org/humanities/us-government-and-civics/us-gov-foundations/us-gov-ideals-of-democracy/v/preamble

Key Constitutional Concepts - Annenberg Classroom www.annenbergclassroom.org/resource/key-constitutional-concepts/

The Declaration of Independence and the Birth of America https://jackmillercenter.org/declaration-independence-birth-america/

Mr. Smith Goes to Washington, 1939

John Adams (HBO Films) 2010

A More Perfect Union: America Becomes a Nation, 1989

The Crossing, 2000

Amistad, 1997

Website Resources

The Supreme Court and Supreme Court Cases http://oyez.com/

Annotation of the Bill of Rights https://www.scribd.com/document/238698937/the-bill-of-rights-annotated

History of the Constitution of the United States http://www.archives.gov/exhibits/charters/constitution_history.html

A Collection of Websites on the Constitution and Early American History http://www.loc.gov/rr/program/bib/ourdocs/Constitution.html

United States House of Representatives http://www.house.gov/

United States Senate http://www.senate.gov/

The White House http://www.whitehouse.gov/

The Library of Congress http://www.loc.gov/index.html

CHAPTER 6

Civil Liberties

1. _____ are the limits on government so that people can freely exercise their rights.

   a. Civil liberties

   b. Civil rights

   c. Selective incorporation

   d. Civil controls

2. Civil require government action to help secure individual rights.

   a. rights

   b. liberties

   c. freedoms

   d. laws

3. Civil _____ restrict government action to protect individual rights.

   a. rights

   b. liberties

   c. freedoms

   d. laws

4. Initially, the Bill of Rights protected against violations of citizens' rights from _____ government(s).

   a. state

   b. federal

   c. state and federal

   d. state and local

5. The Barron v. Baltimore case demonstrates the selective incorporation of what civil liberty?

   a. seizing property

   b. search and seizure

   c. right to bear arms

   d. free-exercise clause

6. Incorporation is defined as extending protections from the Bill of Rights to the state governments, one right at a time.

   a. Concurrent

   b. Majority

   c. Selective

   d. Applicable

7. For what process is the Fourteenth Amendment often the basis?

   a. concurrent incorporation

   b. majority incorporation

   c. applicable incorporation

   d. selective incorporation

8. The Fourteenth Amendment is known as the clause.

   a. due process

   b. clear and present danger

c. free-exercise

d. necessary and proper

9. In what year did the Supreme Court make a classic statement of civil liberties?

a. 1940

b. 1941

c. 1943

d. never

10. What case provides for the selective incorporation of the free exercise of religion?

a. Miranda v. Illinois

b. Benton v. Maryland

c. Cantwell v. Connecticut

d. Powell v. Alabama

11. What case provides for the selective incorporation of the right to free speech?

a. Miranda v. Illinois

b. Benton v. Maryland

c. Gitlow v. New York

d. Powell v. Alabama

12. What case provides for the selective incorporation of the right to remain silent?

a. Miranda v. Illinois

b. Benton v. Maryland

c. Gitlow v. New York

d. Powell v. Alabama

13. What case provides for the selective incorporation of the right to counsel in felony cases?

a. Miranda v. Illinois

b. Gideon v. Wainwright

c. Gitlow v. New York

d. Powell v. Alabama

14. Which of the following rights is not found in the Constitution or Bill of Rights?

a. bear arms

b. abortion

c. cruel and unusual punishment

d. free speech

15. Which Supreme Court case granted women a right to contraceptives?

a. Griswold v. Connecticut

b. Gideon v. Wainwright

c. Gitlow v. New York

d. Powell v. Alabama

16. Which Supreme Court case established a woman's right to choose?

a. Gideon v. Wainwright

b. Roe v. Wade

c. Gitlow v. New York

d. Powell v. Alabama

17. Roe v. Wade overturned a(n) law banning abortion.

a. Texas

b. South Carolina

c. Alabama

d. Mississippi

18. In what year was the Roe v. Wade decision rendered?

a. 1982

b. 1973

c. 1994

d. 1984

19. In 1980, the Court a congressional ban on federal funding for abortions.

a. upheld

b. overturned

c. did not address in the ruling

d. none of these

20. With the Planned Parenthood v. Casey decision, the Court left much discretion in abortions to (the) government(s), so long as they did not go against the Roe decision.

a. state

b. federal

c. local

d. none of these

21. The Planned Parenthood v. Casey decision established a judicial , guiding principles that help governments make judgment calls.

a. standard

b. rule

c. opinion

d. regulation

22. A judicial _____ can be found in the Roe v. Wade case.

    a. standard

    b. rule

    c. opinion

    d. regulation

23. The state that passed the law struck down by Roe v. Wade was

    a. Oklahoma

    b. California

    c. Texas

    d. Arkansas

24. What right did the Lawrence v. Texas case address?

    a. privacy

    b. right to bear arms

    c. free exercise

    d. A cruel and unusual punishment

25. Which case relates to same-sex couples?

    a. Gideon v. Wainwright

    b. Lawrence v. Texas

    c. Gitlow v. New York

    d. Powell v. Alabama

26. Which of the following is not one of the clauses relating to freedom of religion?

    a. free exercise/practice

    b. necessary and proper

c. establishment

d. none of these

27. Where are the rights related to freedom of religion found?

a. First Amendment

b. Second Amendment

c. Eighth and Ninth Amendments

d. Fourth Amendment

28. Which clause says that the government may not interfere in religious practice?

a. free exercise/practice

b. necessary and proper

c. establishment

d. none of these

29. To which clause relates the wall of separation permitting religious freedoms?

a. free exercise/practice

b. necessary and proper

c. establishment

d. none of these

30. Which Court case said starting the school day with a prayer violated the establishment clause?

a. Williams v. Ohio

b. Engel v. Vitale

c. Lemon v. Kurtzman

d. none; the Court ruled it is constitutional

31. The case set a test for judging what government actions are permissible relating to the establishment clause.

    a. Lemon

    b. Engel

    c. Williams

    d. Miranda

32. Which of the following is not part of the Lemon test?

    a. secular purpose

    b. neither advancing nor inhibiting religion

    c. not excessively entangling government in religion

    d. none; these are all parts of the Lemon test

33. Which of the following is allowable, thus not violating the freedom of religion?

    a. children reciting "under God" during the Pledge of Allegiance

    b. prayer at graduation

    c. public school minute of silent prayer or meditation

    d. Christmas displays with secular displays as well

34. Which faith has been predominant in the United States since its founding?

    a. Catholicism

    b. Jewish

    c. Islam

    d. no predominant religion

35. Of what perspective on judging violations of the establishment clause is the Lemon test an example?

    a. accommodation

b. strict separation

c. strict entanglement

d. none of these

36. Which test applies to the free exercise clause?

a. Lemon

b. Engel

c. Sherbert

d. Miranda

37. In the Sherbert case, the Court ruled denying unemployment benefits to someone who was fired for refusing to work on Saturdays for religious reasons was

a. constitutional.

b. unconstitutional.

c. the right thing to do.

d. none of these

38. Which Court case replaced the Sherbert test with a neutrality test?

a. Lawrence v. Texas

b. Employment Division v. Smith

c. Miranda v. Illinois

d. Ohio v. Smith

39. _____ Speech is hostile statements based on someone's personal characteristics.

a. First-degree

b. Second-degree

c. Culturally insensitive

d. Hate

40. When the right to speak out clashes with other rights, like protecting minorities from abusive language, free speech usually

    a. wins.

    b. loses.

    c. ties.

    d. fails to be upheld.

41. In what amendment is the right to free speech guaranteed?

    a. First

    b. Third

    c. Sixth

    d. Seventh

42. Freedom of speech holds a position among rights.

    a. deferential

    b. subsidiary

    c. preferred

    d. none of these

43. The Alien and Sedition Acts relate to which individual freedom?

    a. freedom of speech

    b. freedom of religion

    c. unreasonable search and seizure

    d. no quartering of troops

44. Under the Alien and Sedition Act criticizing the government would lead to

    a. new legislation

    b. changes in laws

c. right to assembly

d. prosecution

45. What test was the result of the Schenck v. US case?

a. necessary and proper

b. clear and present danger

c. constitutional determination of legitimacy

d. none of these

46. Which Supreme Court justice articulated the clear and present danger test?

a. Holmes

b. Roberts

c. Warren

d. O'Connor

47. To which civil liberty applies the clear and present danger test?

a. speech

b. bear arms

c. cruel and unusual punishment

d. right to a grand jury

48. Which of the following is not a form of protected symbolic speech?

a. burning the flag

b. banners advocating drugs at schools

c. wearing armbands to school

d. burning a cross to express views

49. What Court case formed the basis for the test for obscenity in regulating free speech?

    a. Mapp v. Ohio

    b. Miller v. California

    c. Engel v. Vitale

    d. Michigan v. Jones

50. It is generally _____ to prove slander or libel against a public official than an average citizen.

    a. less difficult

    b. more difficult

    c. about the same difficulty

    d. none of these

51. For slander or libel against a public official, what must be proven in the speech?

    a. knowledge

    b. malice

    c. poor fact-checking

    d. none of these

52. In what amendment is the right to bear arms found?

    a. Second

    b. Third

    c. Fifth

    d. Seventh

53. What government was at issue in a recent (2008) Supreme Court decision, which struck down a rule restricting guns to people's homes?

    a. Illinois

b. Virginia

c. District of Columbia

d. South Carolina

54. What case provided for the incorporation of the Second Amendment to lower-level governments?

    a. McDonald v. Chicago

    b. DC v. Heller

    c. Michigan v. Arnold

    d. Mapp v. Ohio

55. Which amendment does not apply to the rights of the accused?

    a. Fourth

    b. Fifth

    c. Seventh

    d. Eighth

56. Relating to the accused's rights, the courts are generally moving away from individual protections and toward law enforcement powers.

    a. enhanced

    b. limited

    c. neutral

    d. none of these

57. Which country leads in the number of incarcerated individuals?

    a. Italy

    b. Denmark

    c. Mexico

    d. US

58. Which case provides the foundation for the exclusionary rule?

    a. Mapp v. Ohio

    b. Miranda v. Arizona

    c. Lawrence v. Texas

    d. Roe v. Wade

59. Which amendment does the exclusionary rule relate to most prominently?

    a. First

    b. Third

    c. Fourth

    d. Seventh

60. The rule says that evidence obtained in an illegal search may not be introduced in a trial.

    a. exclusionary

    b. limited approach

    c. limited inclusion

    d. false pretense

61. The case out which came the exclusionary rule was

    a. Roe v. Wade

    b. Griswold v. Connecticut

    c. Barron v. Baltimore

    d. Mapp v. Ohio

62. The Fourth Amendment is generally referred to as preventing

    a. trials without attorneys.

    b. reading of rights well after arrest.

c. unlawful search and seizure.

d. none of the above

63. Which amendment relates to the rights of individuals at trials?

a. Fourth

b. Fifth

c. Seventh

d. Ninth

64. A citizen's right to a grand jury before a trial is found in what amendment?

a. Fourth

b. Fifth

c. Seventh

d. Ninth

65. A(n) jury is one that does not decide on guilt or innocence but only on whether there is enough evidence for the case to go to trial.

a. grand

b. arraignment

c. attainment

d. golden

66. "You have the right to remain silent" is a famous introduction to what warnings, based on the interpretation of the Fifth Amendment?

a. Miranda

b. Mapp

c. Lawrence

d. None of the above

67. Through the Miranda decision, if a police officer acquires evidence before reading Miranda's warnings, such evidence _____ be admitted in Court.

a. could

b. sometimes could

c. could not

d. none of the above

68. On what amendment is based one's right to an attorney in felony cases?

a. Fourth

b. Fifth

c. Sixth

d. Ninth

69. Originally, one's right to an attorney was only provided in what kind of case?

a. civil

b. capital

c. felony

d. misdemeanor and above

70. Which case granted citizens' rights to an attorney in all felony cases?

a. Gideon v. Wainwright

b. Powell v. Alabama

c. Lawrence v. Texas

d. Jones v. Ohio

71. Debates surrounding the death penalty center around which amendment?

    a. Sixth

    b. Seventh

    c. Eighth

    d. none of the above

72. The Eighth Amendment is typically associated with

    a. unlawful search and seizure.

    b. quartering of troops.

    c. cruel and unusual punishments.

    d. states' rights.

Discussion Questions

1. Define civil liberties.

2. Where is the right to privacy found? Why is it not in the Constitution?

3. Explain the importance of the Fourteenth Amendment.

4. What issues does the right to privacy surround? Discuss current issues facing the Court relating to a person's right to privacy.

5. Discuss the two clauses relating to the right to practice religion.

6. Explain the rights of the accused.

7. Why are some rights, such as speech, sometimes limited? What are the tests for the limitations of some of these rights? Are these hard-and-fast "tests"?

Video Resources

Civil Rights & Liberties: Crash Course Government: #23 Civil Rights and Civil Liberties

https://www.youtube.com/watch?v=kbwsF-A2sTg

The Birth of a Nation (1915) https://www.youtube.com/watch?v=ebtiJH3EOHo

Civil Liberties | The National Constitution Center http://constitution-center.org/interactive-constitution/learning-material/civil-liberties

Korematsu and Civil Liberties www.annenbergclassroom.org/resource/korematsu-civil-liberties/

Milk (2008)

Website Resources

Civil Liberties Monitoring Project http://www.civilliberties.org/

US Department of Homeland Security http://www.dhs.gov/topic/civil-rights-and-civil-liberties

Stanford Journal of Civil Rights & Civil Liberties http://sjcrcl.stanford.edu/home.html

American Civil Liberties Union www.aclu.org

Civil Liberties and Civil Rights http://www.ushistory.org/gov/10.asp

CHAPTER 7

Civil Rights

1. When did Congress outlaw sex discrimination in the Civil Rights Act?

    a. 1964

    b. 1966

    c. 1965

    d. 1968

2. What are rules issued by the president that have the force of law but do not require congressional approval?

    a. presidential orders

    b. executive orders

    c. White House decrees

    d. none of the above

3. What was the Compromise of 1850?

    a. Permitted territories to vote on whether they would be slaves or free.

    b. Local governments would decide whether they would be slaves or free.

    c. Slavery was allowed only in the western states.

    d. all of the above

4. Which 1857 Supreme Court case ruled that the federal government did not have the power to give black men rights rights?

   a. Brown v. Board of Education

   b. Dred Scott v. Sandford

   c. Roe v. Wade

   d. none of the above

5. Which war in American history caused more Americans to lose their lives than in all the other American wars put together?

   a. World War I

   b. Civil War

   c. Korean War

   d. Vietnam War

6. The Fifteenth Amendment excluded which group?

   a. women

   b. blacks

   c. Chinese

   d. none of the above

7. Southern state and local governments reacted to slaves' freedom by passing

   a. anti-sovereignty codes.

   b. nonwhites codes.

   c. black regulations.

   d. black codes.

8. For a time, Congress supported the former slaves. In an effort known as ___, it tried to rebuild the South around a racial justice vision.

   a. the Fourteenth Amendment

b. Reconstruction

c. the Civil Rights Act

d. none of the above

9. Did the Civil Rights Act of 1866 guarantee African Americans the same rights as white Americans?

a. property rights

b. right to participate in politics

c. limited private racial discrimination in hotels, restaurants, and theaters

d. all of the above

10. ___ were allegedly a requirement that voters were literate. In reality, they were a way to restrict black suffrage.

a. Literacy tests

b. Intelligence tests

c. Black voters' tests

d. none of the above

11. In the Civil Rights Cases of 1883, the Supreme Court struck down the Civil Rights Act of 1875, ruling that Congress did not have the authority to stop private discrimination. In what year did Congress finally find a way around this barrier?

a. 1901

b. 2011

c. 1964

d. 1887

12. The white majority built a system of segregation known as ___.

a. Ku Klux Klan

   b. James Crow

   c. Jim Crow

   d. none of the above

13. In what year did the Supreme Court rule, in Plessy v. Ferguson, that there was nothing inherently discriminatory in separating the races?

   a. 1843

   b. 1851

   c. 1896

   d. 1954

14. The percentage of southern students in integrated schools eight years after Brown v. Board of Education was

   a. 74

   b. 6

   c. 1

   d. none

15. What was the plot of the 1915 movie Birth of a Nation?

   a. Social equality for all in America.

   b. Lust-filled black men

   c. The framers of the Constitution.

   d. The Puritans' quest for religious freedom.

16. Beginning in the 1920s, many African Americans left southern agriculture and moved to more lucrative factory jobs in the northern cities—a journey known as the

   a. Northern Migration.

   b. Extradition.

   c. Great Migration.

   d. Great Movement.

17. In 1909, black leaders formed the NAACP. What does this abbreviation stand for?

   a. National Association for the Advancement of Celebrated People

   b. National Association for the Advancement of Christian Patrons

   c. National Association for the Advancement of Colored People

   d. National Association for the Advancement of Christian People

18. In 1961, activists came up with a new tactic. Groups of young people rented Greyhound buses as ___ to protest segregated interstate bus lines and terminals.

   a. Desegregation Riders

   b. Freedom Riders

   c. Freedom for Blacks

   d. freedom activists

19. Which of the following activists was instrumental in the success of the civil rights movement?

   a. Martin L. King

   b. Rosa Parks

   c. A. Philip Randolph

   d. all of the above

20. Martin L. King delivered his famous "I Have a Dream" speech in ___ in Washington, DC.

   a. 1963

   b. 1968

   c. 1995

   d. 1866

21. The Civil Rights Act was passed in what year?

  a. 1991

  b. 1962

  c. 1964

  d. 1865

22. Congress passed the Voting Rights Act in what year?

  a. 1965

  b. 1992

  c. 1967

  d. 1866

23. What is the American ideal often expressed as equality of opportunity?

  a. Give every individual a fair chance at achieving success with the aid of government assistance.

  b. Give every individual a fair chance at achieving success if they can access seed money from parents.

  c. Give every individual a fair chance at achieving success if they are talented and hardworking.

  d. all of the above.

24. When did the new approach of affirmative action emerge in America?

  a. The 1850s and the 1860s

  b. The 1960s and the 1970s

  c. The 1970s and the 1980s

  d. The 1980s and the 1990s

25. Which of the following could a woman do in the early nineteenth century?

  a. vote

b. serve on a jury

c. enter into a contract

d. none of the above

26. When was the first convention for woman suffrage, held at Seneca Falls, that grew directly from the abolition movement?

a. 1848

b. 1891

c. 1898

d. 1937

27. By 1916, an influential political campaign had won full suffrage in fifteen states and partial suffrage in twenty-three others. Women voted in every state of the West and Midwest except

a. Utah.

b. Wyoming.

c. Idaho.

d. New Mexico.

28. Have Latinos taken many of the black civil rights movement tactics and adapted them to their own needs. Did they organize which of the following organizations in 1929?

a. League of United Hispanic American Citizens

b. League of United Latin American Citizens

c. United Latin American League

d. Hispanic League of Freedom

29. Congress passed the _____ in 1882 barring _____ immigrants and declaring them ineligible for citizenship.

a. Japanese Exclusion Act . . . Japanese

b. Chinese Exclusion Act . . . Chinese

c. Vietnamese Exclusion Act . . . Vietnamese

d. Korean Exclusion Act . . . Korean

30. After the Pearl Harbor attack in 1941, President Roosevelt ordered the army to round up Japanese Americans and place them in internment camps. What did they lose as a result of this act of injustice?

a. their liberty

b. their jobs

c. their property and their bank accounts

d. all of the above

31. In 1831, the Supreme Court ruled that Indian tribes were ___.

a. domestic indigenous tribes

b. domestic dependent nations

c. independent countries

d. none of the above

32. The civil rights protests inspired some Native Americans, just as they did so many other groups, to organize a political movement. Which is one such movement?

a. American Indian Sovereignty

b. American Indian United

c. American Indian Movement

d. American Indian Justice

33. Section 504 of the 1973 Rehabilitation Act benefited the disabled. Which piece of legislation did this bill borrow from?

a. the Civil Rights Act of 1964

b. the Constitution

c. the Bill of Rights

d. Civil Rights Act of 1866

34. The movement for same-sex rights began with a riot. In 1969, police raided a ___ gay bar named the Stonewall Inn.

    a. San Francisco

    b. New York City

    c. Los Angeles

    d. Salt Lake City

35. When did the American Psychiatric Association remove homosexuality from its list of mental disorders?

    a. 1949

    b. 1961

    c. 1973

    d. 1999

36. The freedom to participate in the community's full life is also known as

    a. civil liberties

    b. legal rights

    c. executive mandates

    d. civil rights

37. Once civil rights aure won, what is the next job of the public?

    a. protecting them

    b. codifying them

    c. ignoring them

    d. there is no next step

38. One way to view the history of civil rights is as a(n)

    a. easy path

    b. slow march

c. steady march

d. fast run

39. Which of the following is a civil right?

a. voting

b. using public facilities

c. equal economic opportunity

d. all of the above

40. One way to view the history of civil rights is as

a. expanding and contracting

b. moving forward rapidly

c. moving forward slowly

d. moving backward slowly

Discussion Questions

1. Does de facto discrimination still exist today—and, if so, how much?

2. America has made astonishing progress since the days of the civil rights movement; however, significant inequalities remain. What are some of these inequalities?

3. Discuss how Hispanic people come from many different places, each with its own interests and concerns. For example, Cuban Americans are not as concerned with immigration issues as Mexican Americans.

4. Analyze why, unlike Latinos or African Americans, Asian Americans do not form a majority in any electoral districts except Hawaii, although some California districts may soon come close.

5. Discuss the policy of "Indian removal."

6. Discuss the social problems of American Indians. Indian poverty rates are approximately three times as high as the national rates and

stand at 32.2 percent—well above any other American group. Analyze what the US government can do to relieve this dilemma.

Video Resources

USA.gov Channel https://www.youtube.com/usagov1

Icount https://icount.com/

PBS Frontline http://www.pbs.org/wgbh/pages/frontline/view/

Freedom Rider http://www.pbs.org/wgbh/americanexperience/freedomriders/watch

Stonewall Uprising http://www.pbs.org/wgbh/americanexperience/films/stonewall/

We Shall Remain http://www.pbs.org/wgbh/amex/weshallremain/

A Class Apart http://www.pbs.org/wgbh/americanexperience/films/class/

Selma (2014)

The Fight for a Right (2014) www.youtube.com/watch?v=ZOX36uYgMys

Racism, School Desegregation Laws and the Civil Rights Movement in the United States www.youtube.com/watch?v=U9ACS4PgDFA

The Civil Rights Movement: A Cultural Revolution www.memphis.edu/benhooks/documentaries/aculturalrevolution.php

Website Resources

Movement Bibliography: Online Books, Audio, Films & Videos Photos and Images http://www.crmvet.org/biblio-e.htm

Voices of Civil Rights http://www.loc.gov/exhibits/civilrights/

Civil Rights Digital Library http://crdl.usg.edu/?Welcome

The Founder's Constitution http://press-pubs.uchicago.edu/founders/

Political Resources Online http://politicalresources.com/

Online Library of Liberty http://oll.libertyfund.org/

CHAPTER 8

The Legislative Branch

1. A congressional caucus regularly convenes to discuss common interests and consists of which of the following?

   a. House members

   b. Senate members

   c. both House and Senate members

   d. only House leadership

2. All of the following congressional powers could be found in article 1, section 8, except

   a. legal.

   b. financial.

   c. administrative.

   d. national defense.

3. A president needs congressional cooperation primarily to

   a. advance executive policies.

   b. debate public policy.

   c. use the veto process.

   d. limit executive decision-making.

4. A filibuster is a power unique to the

   a. House.

   b. Senate.

   c. House and Senate.

   d. president.

5. A filibuster can only be stopped by a process called

   a. logrolling.

   b. franking.

   c. cloture.

   d. pork-barreling.

6. Congress went from most powerful to increasingly deferential to the White House in the

   a. middle of the twentieth century

   b. early twentieth century

   c. late twentieth century

   d. twenty-first century

7. Today, diversity is more represented in

   a. the House and Senate.

   b. the House.

   c. the Senate.

   d. none of the above

8. A Congress member who cannot promote significant reform would most likely be referred to as a

   a. bass.

   b. minnow.

c. darter.

d. none of the above

9. What crime can the House impeach the president for

a. theft

b. perjury

c. high crimes and misdemeanors

d. murder

10. After the president is impeached the president the trial is held in the

a. White House

b. Senate

c. Supreme Court

d. House of Representatives

11. A central function of the Speaker of the House is to

a. settle all debates.

b. lead the majority party.

c. compromise on key issues.

d. make sure all proposed legislation goes to the president.

12. The second in command in the House is known as the

a. minority leader.

b. majority leader.

c. majority whip.

d. minority whip.

13. Party discipline would most likely be achieved by

a. the Speaker of the House.

b. the majority leader.

   c. the majority party whip.

   d. the minority leader.

14. The Senate position with the longest experience is known as

   a. the vice president.

   b. the president pro tempore.

   c. the majority leader.

   d. the minority leader.

15. The only person who can break a tie in the Senate is the

   a. vice president.

   b. president pro tempore.

   c. minority leader.

   d. whip.

16. The greatest concern about the proposed legislation is that

   a. it will pass.

   b. it will die in a committee.

   c. it will develop into an entirely different piece of legislation.

   d. it will not be debated.

17. The _____ committee is a permanent committee in Congress.

   a. select

   b. standing

   c. conference

   d. social

18. Special committees are often referred to as _____ committees.

   a. select

   b. standing

c. investigative

d. social

19. True or False: The two most important functions of Congress are representation and lawmaking.

20. True or False: The founders created the congressional decision-making process to be fast.

21. True or False: Congressional oversight refers to a congressional committee's monitoring of the executive branch and government agencies to ensure they are acting as Congress intends.

22. True or False: The Senate checks the executive branch through the approval of appointments to the Supreme Court.

23. True or False: The job of confirming presidential appointments belongs to the judiciary.

24. True or False: The reallocation of congressional seats among the states every ten years, following the census, is known as gerrymandering.

25. True or False: The number of representatives with voting privileges in the House of Representatives is currently set at 435 members.

26. True or False: After the census every ten years, House seats are reapportioned among the states to ensure that districts maintain population equality.

27. True or False: The process of redrawing congressional districts to match population shifts in states with more than one representative is called reapportionment.

28. True or False: Redrawing congressional district boundaries to favor a particular group or party is known as gerrymandering.

Discussion Questions

1. What would James Madison say? Develop a comparative perspective about James Madison and how he would view Congress today.

2. What are the central roles of Congress?

3. How do the terms constituents and incumbents relate to congressional power?

4. Is dividing a government a good or bad thing? How can this problem be fixed? What happens when all three branches are controlled by the same party (think FDR)?

Video Resources

Understanding Government: The Legislative Branch (2004)

Cerebellum Corporation

Ken Burns' America: "The Congress" (2004) PBS

Mr. Smith Goes to Washington (1939) Columbia Pictures

How is Congress Doing? Evaluating the Legislative Branch http://bipartisanpolicy.org/event/how-is-congress-doing-evaluating-the-legislative-branch/

Establishment of the Legislative Branch www.c-span.org/video/?295511-1/establishment-legislative-branch

Role and Responsibilities of Legislative Branch www.c-span.org/video/?170130-2/role-responsibilities-legislative-branch&event=170130&playEvent

Website Resources

Congress.org http://www.congress.org/congressorg/directory/congdir.tt

Real Clear Politics http://www.realclearpolitics.com/ welcomead/?ref=http://www.realclearpolitics.com/

270 to Win http://www.270towin.com/

OpenSecrets.org http://www.opensecrets.org/

Government Resources: Legislative Branch Resources - Morningside University http://morningside.libguides.com/government/legislative

Federal Government Resources Research Guide: Legislative Branch - Rutgers Law School http://libguides.law.rutgers.edu/ federal-government-resources/legislative-branch-resources

The Legislative Branch iCivics www.icivics.org/curriculum/ legislative-branch

CHAPTER 9

The Executive Branch

1. The branch of the federal government that has changed the most is
   the
   a. Executive
   b. Legislative
   c. Judicial
   d. all are about the same

2. Presidential power is vaguely defined in
   a. Article 1 of the Constitution
   b. Article 2 of the Constitution
   c. Article 3 of the Constitution
   d. Article 4 of the Constitution

3. Originally, the president would serve a four-year term, which could
   be renewed
   a. indefinitely.
   b. two times.
   c. three times.
   d. four times.

4. The only president who has served more than two terms was

    a. Ronald Reagan.

    b. James Madison.

    c. Franklin Roosevelt.

    d. Thomas Jefferson.

5. Which amendment bars a president from serving a third term?

    a. the Twenty-second

    b. the Twenty-third

    c. the Twenty-fourth

    d. the Nineteenth

6. The agreed-on way to elect the president is

    a. by Congress.

    b. through the Electoral College.

    c. by the courts.

    d. by the political parties.

7. In the Electoral College, each state's number of votes is _____ its congressional delegation.

    a. greater than

    b. less than

    c. equal to

    d. significantly less than

8. Who determines how electors to the Electoral College are chosen?

    a. states

    b. Congress

    c. President

    d. Political Parties

9. In order to win the presidency, one must win

    a. the Electoral College and popular vote.

    b. the popular vote.

    c. the Electoral College.

    d. a simple plurality in the Electoral College.

10. Executive expressed powers include all of the following except

    a. commander in chief.

    b. power to declare war.

    c. power to make treaties.

    d. power to grant pardons.

11. Treaty ratification can only occur with

    a. House approval.

    b. judicial approval.

    c. Senate approval.

    d. bureaucratic approval.

12. Senatorial approval of a treaty requires

    a. one-third support

    b. two-thirds support

    c. three-quarters support

    d. unanimous support

13. The idea that the executive branch can issue a rule on congressional legislation is known as

    a. proscribed powers.

    b. legislative power.

    c. delegated powers.

    d. enumerated powers.

14. The three forms of presidential powers are

    a. expressed, reserved, and formal.

    b. expressed, delegated, and reserved.

    c. expressed, delegated, and inherent.

    d. inherent, reserved, and delegated.

15. Powers vaguely reflected in Article 2 of the Constitution are known as

    a. reserved powers.

    b. expressed powers.

    c. inherent powers.

    d. de facto powers.

16. Holding enemy combatants without a hearing can be traced to which executive power?

    a. reserved

    b. inherent

    c. delegated

    d. expressed

17. The _____ can determine whether the president exceeded the scope of inherent powers.

    a. Supreme Court

    b. House

    c. Senate

    d. Bureaucracy

18. Many parliamentary systems grant their executives which of the following?

    a. right to use emergency powers

    b. right to use partial line-item vetoes

c. right to introduce budgets

d. all of the above

19. Presidents are elected _____ via the Electoral College.

a. indirectly

b. directly

c. by plurality

d. by national popular vote

20. Executive power generally _____during crises.

a. diminishes

b. expands

c. stays the same

d. completely changes

21. The Alien and Sedition Acts can be traced to which presidency?

a. John Adams

b. George Washington

c. Thomas Jefferson

d. James Madison

22. The Alien and Sedition Acts were considered controversial because they punished false and scandalous speech, but they also could be viewed as an attack on which amendment?

a. First

b. Second

c. Third

d. Fourth

23. The idea that no other branch can check the president is known as the

a. supremacy theory.

b. unitary executive theory.

c. imperial theory.

d. take care clause.

24. The idea that the president could demand swift and even secretive action is supported by

a. unitary executive theory.

b. legislative theory.

c. inherent theory.

d. pluralist theory.

25. The unitary executive theory can be viewed as

a. a threat to the system of checks and balances.

b. an important way to change governmental roles.

c. a way for the president to serve more than two terms.

d. a way for Congress to override the president.

26. The idea that an executive could possibly change a republic into an empire is directly related to which of the following theories?

a. legislative

b. imperial

c. pluralist

d. majoritarian

27. Presidents are highly vulnerable in relation to

a. foreign affairs.

b. domestic issues.

c. legislative issues.

d. judicial issues.

28. The president presides over the world's largest fighting force and is otherwise known as the

a. commander in chief.

b. chief legislator.

c. chief diplomat.

d. chief executive.

29. Free trade agreements, global warming concerns, and the Middle East concerns all require the use of

a. force.

b. economic sanctions.

c. diplomacy.

d. boycotts.

30. The president can act as a _____ and recommend and veto measures from Congress.

a. chief legislator

b. chief diplomat

c. chief custodian

d. commander in chief

31. Prior to World War II, what type of standing army did the United States have?

a. large

b. small

c. strong

d. weak

32. After World War II, what type of standing army did the United States have?

    a. small

    b. large

    c. weak

    d. all-male

33. An annual event where the president addresses the nation is called

    a. the annual talk.

    b. the State of the Union address.

    c. the Executive Talk.

    d. the State of Affairs Talk.

34. Which of the following can formally propose a law?

    a. President

    b. Congress

    c. the Supreme Court

    d. both a and b

35. _____is the presidential power to block an act of Congress by refusing to sign it.

    a. Executive power

    b. Legislative power

    c. Veto power

    d. Take care clause power

Discussion Questions

1. What is the difference between a leader and a manager, and how does that relate to the modern presidency?

2. Has presidential power gone too far in the fight against terrorism?

3. Will there be a female president in the next 10–20 years, and why?

4. Should the term natural-born citizen be removed as a requirement to run for the presidency?

Video Resources

American Presidents (2005) History Channel

American Presidents (2012) Cerebellum Corporation

American Presidents (2012) Software Lab

Role and Responsibilities of Executive Branch www.c-span.org/video/? 170130-1/role-responsibilities-executive-branch&event=170130&playEvent

Scholar Exchange: The Presidency and the Executive Branch With Holly Frey - Constitution Center http://constitutioncenter.org/interactive-constitution/educational-video/scholar-exchange-the-presidency-and-the-executive-branch-with-holly-frey

H.R. 1: Strengthening Ethics Rules for the Executive Branch http://oversight.house.gov/legislation/hearings/hr-1-strengthening-ethics-rules-for-the-executive-branch

Website Resources

The White House http://whitehouse.gov and http://www.whitehouse.gov/about/presidents

National Archives Executive Orders http://www.archives.gov/federal-register/executive-orders

National Archives Executive Orders Disposition Tables Index http://www.archives.gov/federal-register/executive-orders/disposition.html

Maps of War http://www.mapsofwar.com/

CHAPTER 10

The Judicial Branch

1. Appellate courts hear cases from the

   a. Supreme Court.

   b. lower courts.

   c. courts of dual jurisdiction.

   d. courts of upper jurisdiction.

2. According to Alexander Hamilton, the weakest of the three branches of government was

   a. Congress.

   b. the presidency.

   c. the judiciary

   d. the bureaucracy.

3. The use of a third party to solve a legal dispute most likely refers to the process called

   a. litigation.

   b. mediation.

   c. civic relations.

   d. adjudication.

4. One of the unusual things about the courts is that

   a. there have always been nine Supreme Court justices.

   b. the Constitution never specified the number of Supreme Court justices.

   c. Congress has an insignificant role in shaping the courts.

   d. the president has a minimal role in influencing who is on the courts.

5. The concept of judicial federalism means

   a. that the US has one main court system.

   b. that the courts should be judicious in making relevant decisions.

   c. that there is both a federal and a state court system in the United States.

   d. that state courts are stronger than federal courts.

6. The ultimate arbiter of all cases is the

   a. trial court.

   b. superior court.

   c. US Supreme Court.

   d. federal court.

7. In what year was the Supreme Court set at nine justices?

   a. 1797

   b. 1812

   c. 1869

   d. 1962

8. Most state judges

   a. are appointed for life.

   b. are selected by state legislatures.

c. are elected by the public.

d. have terms that are not renewable.

9. The main ways to select a judge are

a. by public vote.

b. by governor's appointment.

c. by merit committees.

d. all of the above

10. Acts of terror, insider trading, and immigration would be heard by

a. state trial courts.

b. federal trial courts.

c. state appeals court.

d. state supreme court.

11. A district court is a

a. state appellate court.

b. state trial court.

c. federal trial court.

d. state supreme court.

12. Texas and California have _____than other states.

a. fewer district courts

b. more district courts

c. more powerful district courts

d. weaker district courts

13. District court judges are appointed by the

a. people.

b. governor.

c. president.

d. state legislature.

14. The role of the circuit courts is to

    a. review the trial record of cases decided in district court.

    b. review the trial record of cases decided in state trial courts.

    c. review the trial record of cases decided in state appellate courts.

    d. review the record of cases decided in mediation.

15. There are _____ federal appellate courts.

    a. 94

    b. 10

    c. 13

    d. 75

16. The main difference between the federal appellate court and the federal district court is that

    a. there are more federal appellate courts.

    b. federal appellate courts use juries.

    c. federal appellate courts do not use juries or cross-examination.

    d. federal district courts do not allow cross-examination.

17. Circuit courts review cases decided in

    a. Supreme Court

    b. District Courts

    c. Bankruptcy Courts

    d. Military Courts

18. Specialized courts hear cases on

    a. immigration.

b. tax disputes.

c. treason.

d. civil rights.

19. Specialized court judges differ from regular federal judges in that

    a. They are older than federal judges.

    b. they are not appointed for life.

    c. they do not require Senate confirmation.

    d. they must be appointed by the governor.

20. If there were a breach of justice by a military member, that case would be heard by

    a. a district court judge.

    b. a military judge.

    c. an appellate court.

    d. a state judge.

21. The principle that enables the courts to check the other two branches of government is known as

    a. legal authority.

    b. judicial autonomy.

    c. judicial review.

    d. statutory relief.

22. The principle of judicial review is traced back to the case of

    a. McCullough v. Maryland.

    b. Gibbons v. Ogden.

    c. Marbury v. Madison.

    d. Plessy v. Ferguson.

23. Judicial review allows the courts to

    a. check only Congress if it has exceeded constitutional authority.

    b. check the executive and legislative branches if they have exceeded constitutional authority.

    c. check only the executive branch if it has exceeded constitutional authority.

    d. check the military.

24. Judicial review is _____ in the Constitution.

    a. clearly mentioned

    b. vaguely mentioned

    c. not mentioned

    d. reflected through the Judiciary Act of 1789

25. The statement "When there is doubt about what the Constitution holds or implies, the Supreme Court makes the call" refers to the principle of

    a. stare decisis.

    b. judicial review.

    c. certiorari.

    d. senatorial courtesy.

26. The fact that the Supreme Court has struck down statutes that supported segregation policy is a form of

    a. judicial activism.

    b. legal rationalism.

    c. judicial restraint.

    d. strict constructionism.

27. The idea that the Supreme Court can take a vigorous or active approach when reviewing the other governmental branches is a form of

    a. judicial activism.

    b. judicial restraint.

    c. legal activism.

    d. common law practice.

28. The idea that the Court should overturn the elected branches of government reluctantly is called

    a. judicial reproach.

    b. judicial restraint.

    c. judicial activism.

    d. loose constructionism.

29. The early English legal system was known as

    a. majority rule.

    b. the Magna Carte.

    c. common law.

    d. common precedent.

30. Judicial cases today may be important tomorrow because they establish the concept of

    a. judicial review.

    b. precedent.

    c. legal formation.

    d. civil law.

31. A judge that makes a legal decision on a case today may look at past case law and follow the concept of

    a. precedent.

    b. civil law.

    c. criminal law.

    d. home rule.

32. A person charged with theft will face the rules and consequences under

    a. criminal law.

    b. civil law.

    c. humanitarian law.

    d. common law.

33. The person bringing the suit in a civil case is called the

    a. prosecutor.

    b. litigator.

    c. defendant.

    d. plaintiff.

34. The person being sued in a civil case is known as the

    a. respondent.

    b. plaintiff.

    c. defendant.

    d. petitioner.

35. Federal courts differ from the executive and legislative branches of government because they

    a. are above politics.

    b. serve more extended periods.

c. are all from one political party.

d. do not have an electoral base.

36. Supreme Court justices are in session

    a. all year round.

    b. for nine months.

    c. for six months.

    d. for eleven months.

37. A brief submitted by a person or group that is not a direct party to the case is called

    a. amicus curiae.

    b. third-party brief.

    c. legal extension.

    d. case law.

38. The Supreme Court process of selecting a case is known as

    a. a gang of four.

    b. rule of four.

    c. the process of advice and consent.

    d. rule of twelve.

39. Which of the following is essential for having a case heard by the Supreme Court?

    a. standing

    b. legitimate controversy

    c. no moot cases

    d. all of the above

40. Someone adversely affected or suffering imminent harm would be able to satisfy the concept of

    a. due process.

    b. standing.

    c. amicus curiae.

    d. justiciability.

41. The official statement of the Court is known as

    a. the dissent.

    b. the majority opinion.

    c. the concurring opinion.

    d. the remand.

42. A justice that agrees with the majority opinion but for different reasons is known as

    a. an opposite opinion.

    b. a concurring opinion.

    c. a dissenting opinion.

    d. a circulatory opinion.

43. A statement on behalf of the justices voting in the minority is called the

    a. dissent.

    b. concurring opinion.

    c. differing opinion.

    d. legal treatise.

44. Justices are guided by the concept of _____in making legal decisions.

    a. common law.

    b. stare decisis.

    c. devolution.

    d. rule of four.

45. "Stand by the things decided" is the definition for which Latin term?

    a. writ of certiorari

    b. writ of mandamus

    c. writ of habeas corpus

    d. stare decisis

46. A judge who observes a living and changing Constitution is known as a

    a. theorist.

    b. pragmatist.

    c. rationalist.

    d. legalist.

47. A judge who literally interprets the Constitution literally is known as a(n)

    a. legalist.

    b. loose constructionist.

    c. originalist.

    d. pragmatist.

48. The case of Marbury v. Madison and the judicial review principle was set forth by which Supreme Court justice?

    a. Robert Taney

    b. John Marshall

    c. Hugo Black

    d. John Marshall Harlan

49. McCulloch v. Maryland was essential to court development because

    a. it allowed the federal government to tax a state.

    b. it evoked the principle of the good faith and credit clause.

    c. it evoked the necessary and proper clause to block Maryland's state from taxing the bank of the United States.

    d. it allowed states to create complex interstate compacts.

50. The outcome of McCulloch v. Maryland affirmed the principle that

    a. the federal government is superior to state governments.

    b. states are superior to the federal government in most instances.

    c. state and federal power are equal.

    d. states can use state mandates to trump federal power.

51. The famous case that denied civil rights to former slaves was known as

    a. Plessy v. Ferguson.

    b. Dred Scott v. Sandford.

    c. Marbury v. Madison.

    d. Guinn v. United States.

52. A fundamental principle in the Dred Scott case was that slaves could not sue because

    a. they did not have enough money.

    b. they lacked standing to sue.

    c. their cases were only common law concerns.

    d. their cases were not federal.

53. The idea that a corporation was viewed as a legal person meant

    a. that corporations did not have to pay federal taxes.

    b. that corporations were protected under the equal protection clause of the Thirteenth Amendment.

  c. that corporations were protected under the equal protection clause of the Fourteenth Amendment.

  d. that corporations could use their own lawyers during the trial.

54. Black equality was promoted through which amendments?

  a. Seven, Eight, and Nine

  b. Thirteen, Fourteen, and Fifteen

  c. One, Two, and Three

  d. Five, Eight, and Nine

55. The outcome of Plessy v. Ferguson was

  a. fair and equal treatment for all people.

  b. the promotion of desegregation with all deliberate speed.

  c. the separate but equal policy.

  d. the development of a color-blind society.

56. The outcome of Schenck v. United States was

  a. the equal protection clause.

  b. the clear and present danger test.

  c. the due process clause.

  d. the grave and probable danger test.

57. The case that forced Japanese Americans into internment camps during World War II was

  a. Korematsu v. US.

  b. Schenck v. US.

  c. Gitlow v. New York.

  d. Plessy v. Ferguson.

58. The Korematsu case was significant because it was

   a. one of the first cases to use the strict scrutiny test.

   b. one of the first cases to use the clear and present danger test.

   c. one of the first cases to use the grave and probable danger test.

   d. one of the first cases to use the adverse tendency rule.

59. The case that overturned Plessy v. Ferguson was

   a. Gitlow v. New York.

   b. Guinn v. United States.

   c. Korematsu v. United States.

   d. Brown v. Board

60. The court in Brown v. Board stated that

   a. separate schools are inherently unequal.

   b. separate facilities are inherently unequal.

   c. separate movie theaters are inherently unequal.

   d. separate restrooms are inherently unequal.

61. Mapp v. Ohio addressed concerns over the

   a. Eighth Amendment.

   b. Fourth Amendment.

   c. Third Amendment.

   d. Sixth Amendment.

62. Gideon v. Wainwright was one of the first in a series of landmark judicial decisions addressing

   a. the right to bear arms.

   b. the right of free speech.

c. the rights of defendants in criminal proceedings.

d. the rights of immigrant workers.

63. The case that struck down a Texas law outlawing abortion was

a. Roe v. Wade.

b. Mapp v. Ohio.

c. Gideon v. Wainwright.

d. Miranda v. Arizona.

64. The case that addressed the president's right to use executive privilege was

a. Roe v. Wade.

b. US v. Nixon.

c. US v. Ford.

d. Bush v. Gore.

65. The idea that the president can withhold sensitive national security information from Congress or the courts is known as an

a. executive order.

b. executive pardon.

c. executive privilege.

d. executive agreement.

66. Obergefell v. Hodges brought _____ to the Supreme Court.

a. tax evasion

b. same-sex marriage

c. health benefits

d. death rights

67. The Court used the _____ amendment in deciding Obergefell v. Hodges.

   a. 1st

   b. 11th

   c. 14th

   d. 22nd

Discussion Questions

1. What makes a good judge?

2. Evaluate whether the courts were too influential in Bush v. Gore.

3. Should the US government have a mandated health plan?

4. Should justices have term limits? How long should the term be? Should every president be allowed to nominate a Supreme Court justice? How would that work?

Video Resources

Noah Feldman and Jeffrey Toobin: The Supreme Court Then and Now (2010) 92nd Street Y

The Supreme Court DVD Series (2007) Ambrose Video Publishing

Stare decisis and precedent in the Supreme Court https://www.khanacademy.org/humanities/ap-us-government-and-politics/interactions-among-branches-of-government/legitimacy-of-the-judicial-branch/v/stare-decisis-and-precedent-in-the-supreme-court

Ruth Bader Ginsburg, Brooklyn's Own Supreme Court Justice https://www.youtube.com/watch?v=AsbjuX0YxzY

Court Role and Structure www.uscourts.gov/about-federal-courts/court-role-and-structure

Abbout the Supreme Court https://www.courts.state.wy.us/supreme-court/about-the-supreme-court/

Website Resources

The Supreme Court of the United States http://www.supremecourt.gov/ and

http://www.supremecourt.gov/about/biographies.aspx

United States Courts http://www.uscourts.gov

The Supreme Court Historical Society http://www.supremecourthistory.org

Supreme Court www.oyez.org

CHAPTER 11

Public opinion, campaigns, and elections

1. The first presidential caucus of the season is held in
   a. New Hampshire
   b. Massachusetts
   c. Iowa
   d. California

2. What would be a reason for a special election?
   a. officeholder dies
   b. President does not like office holder
   c. voters ask for one
   d. governor asks for one

3. What percentage of the House is elected every two years?
   a. 33%
   b. 50%
   c. 75%
   d. 100%

4. How often is the president elected?

    a. every four years

    b. every six years

    c. every eight years

    d. when he calls an election

5. The state governs the ___and ___ of elections.

    a. "place"… "manner"

    b. "time"… "day"

    c. "practice"… "application"

    d. none of the above

6. The state governs the ___and ___ of elections.

    a. "time"… "manner"

    b. "time"… "day"

    c. "practice"… "application"

    d. none of the above

7. The date of the primary is set by the

    a. state

    b. political party

    c. president

    d. Congress

8. When was the date of elections set?

    a. 1845

    b. 1951

    c. 1917

    d. 1983

9. In parliamentary democracies, what is the usual time in which an election must be held?

    a. three years

    b. four years

    c. five years

    d. six years

10. What month are Senate elections held?

    a. March

    b. November

    c. January

    d. September

11. What day of the week do Americans vote for House members?

    a. Saturday

    b. Friday

    c. Wednesday

    d. Tuesday

12. In what year are House elections held?

    a. even-numbered years

    b. years divisible by three

    c. years divisible by five

    d. odd-numbered years

13. When is election day for House members?

    a. first Tuesday after first Monday in November of every even-numbered year

    b. first Wednesday after first Monday in November of every even-numbered year

c. first Tuesday after first Thursday in November of every even-numbered year

d. first Tuesday after first Monday in November of every odd-numbered year

14. How much of the Senate is elected every two years?

a. 100%

b. half

c. one-fourth

d. one-third

15. United States senators' term is ___ years; that's one of the ___ elected terms in the world.

a. two… shortest

b. four… quickest

c. six… longest

d. none of the above

16. All American national elections are on a fixed cycle (except when an officeholder resigns or dies). Which of the following dire situations would affect this schedule?

a. war

b. economic collapse

c. terrorist attacks

d. none of the above

17. A prime minister once remarked: "In your system, you guys campaign for 24 hours a day, every day for two years. You know, politics is one thing, but we have to run a government." Which was the origin country of this politician?

a. Belgium

b. France

c. Canada

d. Great Britain

18. The United States was the ___ nation to choose its chief executive by popular election.

a. first

b. second

c. twentieth

d. fourth

19. Today, how many states elect judges?

a. 20

b. 39

c. 50

d. 10

20. The US system sets strict limits on individual donations: no one may contribute more than ___ to any individual candidate.

a. $2,700

b. $3.5 million

c. $45,000

d. $500

21. Parties generally nominate candidates from which office for president?

a. attorney general

b. secretary of state

c. governor

d. House

22. ___ is the date on the primary calendar when most states hold primaries and caucuses on the same day.

    a. Super Tuesday

    b. Super Election Day

    c. Super Primaries and Caucuses Day

    d. none of the above

23. Which event typically has the effect of creating an increase in the poll numbers for a presidential candidate?

    a. political party convention

    b. rock concert

    c. graduation ceremony

    d. none of the above

24. ___ refers to a system under which the winning candidate receives all the delegates for that state.

    a. Winner-take-all system

    b. Proportional representation

    c. Demographic system

    d. none of the above

25. A system of ___ allocates delegates based on the proportion of the vote a candidate wins.

    a. winner-take-all

    b. demographics

    c. proportional representation

    d. none of the above

26. Traditionally, which party has adhered to the winner-take-all system?

    a. Republicans

b. Democrats

c. Green Party

d. none of the above

27. Traditionally, which party has adhered to the proportional representation system?

a. Republicans

b. Social Party

c. Democrats

d. all of the above

28. During the primary season, candidates must

a. raise as much money as possible

b. visit as many states as possible

c. make a solid first impression

d. avoid television commercials

29. When members of a political party get together before a general election to choose delegates to the convention, they are attending a

a. primary

b. general election meeting

c. caucus

d. convention planning meeting

30. When only party members can cast a vote in the primary, it is known as a(n)

a. caucus

b. open primary

c. closed primary

d. private vote

31. When any eligible voter can vote in a primary, it is known as a(n)

    a. caucus

    b. closed primary

    c. public vote

    d. open primary

32. Party officials hope to have a candidate by

    a. Labor Day

    b. Super Tuesday

    c. Fourth of July

    d. Memorial Day

33. Candidates running in the primary are talking to more _____ voters and then to more _____ voters in the general election.

    a. centrist; ideologically driven

    b. ideologically driven; centrist

    c. liberal; conservative

    d. conservative; liberal

34. ___ refers to the tendency for members of Congress to win reelection in overwhelming numbers.

    a. Nepotism advantage

    b. Incumbency advantage

    c. Insider advantage

    d. none of the above

35. What are midterm elections?

    a. Elections held in the middle of the year.

    b. Elections held in the middle of each term.

    c. Elections held in a nonpresidential election year.

    d. none of the above

Discussion Questions

1. Explain the concept of groupthink.

2. What conditions must be met for public opinion to guide the government?

3. Discuss the difference between a push poll and a scientific survey.

4. Why is it essential for survey research to be random?

5. Compare the boomerang and bandwagon effects.

6. Discuss factors affecting how one thinks politically.

7. Why are those better educated more likely to be involved? Should the government work to teach all citizens about civic duty? How would they do so?

8. How do friends and family influence voting behavior? How about the neighborhood? Civic organizations?

Video Resources

Media Education Foundation http://www.mediaed.org/

"Poll Bearers," from The Daily Show http://www.cc.com/video-clips/xd8n18/the-daily-show-with-jon-stewart-poll-bearers

Icount https://icount.com/

PBS Frontline http://www.pbs.org/wgbh/pages/frontline/view/

Firing Line Debates https://www.hoover.org/library-archives/collections/firing-line

Art as Propaganda: The Nazi Degenerate Art Exhibit www.facinghistory.org/resource-library/video/art-propaganda-nazi-degenerate-art-exhibit

Why media should think twice about public-opinion polls: Panel discussion http://journalistsresource.org/politics-and-government/criticism-media-use-public-opinion-polls/

Why policy decisions may not reflect perceived public opinion - Khan Academy www.khanacademy.org/humanities/ap-us-government-and-politics/american-political-ideologies-and-beliefs/evaluating-public-opinion-data/v/why-policy-decisions-may-not-reflect-perceived-public-opinion

Bot or not? How fake social media accounts could influence voting www.pbs.org/newshour/extra/lessons-plans/lesson-plan-how-to-use-social-media-for-social-good/

The Nature of Public Opinion https://courses.lumenlearning.com/os-government2e/chapter/the-nature-of-public-opinion/

Does Public Opinion Matter? World Attitudes on Global Governance www.cfr.org/event/does-public-opinion-matter-world-attitudes-global-governance-0

Website Resources

Public Agenda Online http://www.publicagenda.org/

Center for Civic Engagement http://www.engage.northwestern.edu

Political Resources Online http://politicalresources.com/

Roper Center for Public Opinion Research https://ropercenter.cornell.edu/

Online Library of Liberty http://oll.libertyfund.org/

Polling Report http://pollingreport.com/

Gallup www.gallup.com

Pew Research Center for the People and the Press http://www.people-press.org/

CNN Politics Polling Center http://www.cnn.com/POLITICS/polling-center/index.html

CHAPTER 12

Bureaucracy

1. The bureaucracy, compared to Congress,

   a. is older.

   b. is younger.

   c. is much more diverse.

   d. is more educated.

2. The practice, by which political winners reward their supporters with government jobs and contracts, is known as

   a. the spoils system.

   b. pandering.

   c. pay-for-play.

   d. the nepotism system.

3. The act of Congress requiring the federal government to hire well-qualified public servants in 1883 was

   a. the Hatch.

   b. the Hire Qualified Government Workers Act of 1883.

   c. the McCain-Feingold Act.

   d. the Pendleton Civil Service Act.

4. A transparent chain of command, where all employees know who their supervisors are and who reports to them, is an example of a

   a. hierarchy.

   b. merit-based system.

   c. spoils system.

   d. patronage.

5. The ultimate purpose of creating a professional merit-based civil service system is to

   a. give jobs to friends

   b. hire well-qualified individuals

   c. win elections

   d. hire party members

6. The effort to outlaw all liquor under Prohibition created a new law enforcement agency in the

   a. Church of Jesus Christ of Latter-day Saints.

   b. Department of the Interior.

   c. Federal Bureau of Investigation.

   d. Department of the Treasury.

7. The Federal Reserve was created

   a. to stabilize banking.

   b. to save money.

   c. to prepare for World War I.

   d. to build Fort Knox.

8. Laws written by Congress are typically

   a. very precise.

   b. consensual.

c. detailed.

d. vague.

9. After an agency has devised a rule, it sends the rule to the _____ for approval.

a. Office of Rule Enforcement

b. General Accounting Office

c. Federal Register

d. Office of Management and Budget

10. The daily journal of the federal government is

a. The Federal Register.

b. The New York Times.

c. The Journal of Rules.

d. The Hill.

11. Because bureaucracies are so rule-based, they

a. make decisions that usually only serve public employees.

b. make poor decisions.

c. make conflicting and confusing decisions.

d. make decisions with accountability and equality, but also with much bureaucratic red tape.

12. Bureaucracies exist

a. in both the private and public sectors.

b. only in government.

c. at the federal level.

d. in Europe, for the most part.

13. The final rule is published in the

    a. Federal Rule Book

    b. Federal Guidelines

    c. Federal Bureaucracy Guidelines

    d. Federal Register

14. Bureaucracies touch

    a. every aspect of our lives.

    b. very little of our day-to-day existence.

    c. the economy, mainly.

    d. social issues, mainly.

15. Which of the following is an example of a federal agency designed to serve a clientele group?

    a. State Department

    b. Department of Justice

    c. Homeland Security

    d. Agriculture

16. President George Washington's administration had all of the following cabinet departments except

    a. Interior.

    b. War.

    c. State.

    d. Treasury.

17. All of the following are events that led to growth in the federal bureaucracy except

    a. 9/11.

    b. The Emancipation Proclamation.

c. WWII.

d. The Great Depression.

18. The cabinet secretary who sits farthest away from the president at cabinet meetings is

a. Secretary of Defense.

b. Secretary of Treasury.

c. Secretary of Homeland Security.

d. Secretary of State.

19. Who defined bureaucracy as "an organization where tasks are divided among technical specialists who devote their full working capacity to the organization and whose activities are coordinated by rational rules, hierarchy and written documents"

a. Douglas North

b. Karl Marx

c. Max Weber

d. None of the above.

20. True or False: According to Weber, bureaucracy was a decline compared to previous societal forms of political management and it was necessary to resolve many political issues in current societies

21. True or False: Bureaucracy has not been a central topic of study in political science over the last centuries.

22. According to Bernard Manin, elections tend to create

a. democracies

b. monarchies

c. aristocracies

d. None of the above

23. True or False: According to Bernard Manin, elections tend to create aristocracies, since they select candidates that prove to have the politically relevant qualities and that are deemed superior by the dominant values in the culture.

24. Which article of the United States Constitution included political patronage?

    a. Article 1

    b. Article 2

    c. Article 4

    d. Article 5

25. True or False: U.S. citizens want to know how governments are using the people's money, especially concerning taxpayer funds

Discussion Questions

1. How many bureaucracies do you think you deal with in a day?

2. Who controls the bureaucracy?

3. Should bureaucrats be elected?

4. Bureaucrats have a negative perception. Is this deserved or exaggerated?

5. Do bureaucrats do good or is it all bad?

Video Resources

PBS Frontline

Judicial Branch and the Federal Bureaucracy - Bill of Rights Institute http://billofrightsinstitute.org/videos/judicial-branch-and-the-federal-bureaucracy-apgov-prep-webinar

Bureaucracy - A documentary by Dr Richard Cole www.youtube.com/watch?v=B_nsZlcC12g

Too Big to Fail (2011) HBO Films

Apollo 13 (1995)

Brazil (1985)

Yes, Minister (1980–1984) BBC

Yes, Prime Minister (1986–1988) BBC

The Trial (1962)

Catch-22 (1970)

Dr. Strangelove or: How I Learned to Stop Worrying and Love the Bomb (1964)

Website Resources

Federal Register https://www.federalregister.gov/

USA.gov http://www.usa.gov/

Who are the bureaucrats? http://www.ushistory.org/gov/8c.asp

What is the Federal Bureaucracy? https://www.youtube.com/watch?v=PZg1gp2VZDo

Bureaucracy Basics: Crash Course Government and Politics #15 https://www.youtube.com/watch?v=I8EQAnKntLs

CHAPTER 13

Political Parties and Interest Group

1. James Madison warned against interest groups in Federalist no. ____
   a. 5.
   b. 7.
   c. 10.
   d. 25.

2. Madison refers to interest groups in the Federalist no. 10 as
   a. lobbyists.
   b. factions.
   c. special interests.
   d. political parties.

3. Which of the following terms does not refer to a group primarily interested in gaining government support to pursue its specific policy goals?
   a. allied group
   b. special interest group
   c. faction
   d. interest group

4. An interest group is defined as

   a. an organization whose goal is to influence citizens.

   b. an organization whose goal is to get members elected to office.

   c. an organization whose goal is to disrupt the lawmaking process.

   d. an organization whose goal is to influence the government.

5. The two crucial elements in the definition of an interest group are

   a. membership and money.

   b. organization and influence.

   c. bribery and blackmail.

   d. persuasion and information.

6. A _____ is an individual who contacts government officials on behalf of a particular cause or issue.

   a. lobbyist

   b. constituent

   c. member of Congress

   d. specialist

7. One of the threats of strict or intense partisanship is that it could lead to

   a. increased participation.

   b. effective conflict.

   c. a decrease in ideological thinking.

   d. increased apathy.

8. Which of the following is an example of a membership group?

   a. AARP

   b. Lockheed-Martin

c. American Israel Public Affairs Committee

d. US Chamber of Commerce

9. Which of the following is not a primary function of interest groups?

   a. Informing members about political developments.

   b. Buying the votes of members of Congress.

   c. Communicating members' views to government officials.

   d. Mobilizing the public.

10. Which branch of government do lobbyists contact to convey their opinions and push their policy priorities?

   a. executive branch

   b. legislative branch

   c. judicial branch

   d. all of the above

11. For an interest group to be successful, it must

   a. inform members about political developments.

   b. communicate members' views to government officials.

   c. mobilize the public.

   d. all of the above.

12. When an issue arises in Washington that is of interest to a group, the group tends to

   a. Gain more members.

   b. Boost its spending.

   c. Get ignored by legislators.

   d. both a and c

13. On high-profile issues like climate change, lobbying

    a. Has little effect on the views of members of Congress.

    b. Has great potential to change the views of members of Congress.

    c. Has an effect on some members and no effect on other members of Congress, regardless of party.

    d. Has little effect on members of Congress who are Democrats, but great effect on members of Congress who are Republicans.

14. Beginning in the mid-1960s, the number of lobbyists

    a. increased dramatically.

    b. decreased dramatically.

    c. stayed the same as pre-1960s.

    d. decreased only slightly.

15. In Federalist no. 10, Madison suggests how to prevent factions from killing off the popular government is to

    a. outlaw them.

    b. increase the number of them.

    c. ignore them.

    d. limit how many there can be.

16. Interest groups today represent

    a. virtually every political or social topic and concern.

    b. a limited number of political or social groups.

    c. a tiny number of wealthy individuals.

    d. none of the above

17. "An interest group primarily organized with voluntary members, often with a nonprofit or public advocacy focus" is a good definition for a

   a. membership group.

   b. lobbying coalition.

   c. special interest.

   d. faction.

18. A _____ is a group of lobbyists working on related topics or a specific legislative proposal.

   a. special interest

   b. faction

   c. membership group

   d. lobbying coalition

19. When interest groups mobilize the public to do something on their behalf, this includes actions such as

   a. letter writing.

   b. protesting.

   c. contributing funds.

   d. all of the above

20. When interest groups mobilize the public, they typically reach out through

   a. TV ads.

   b. Facebook posts.

   c. mailgram alerts.

   d. all of the above

21. Pluralism is defined as

a. an open, participatory style of government in which many different interests are represented.

b. a closed system of government in which only a handful of individuals may participate.

c. a system that can only benefit the wealthy.

d. an open style of government in which only a few individuals are represented.

22. Which of the following theories best explains the bank bailouts of 2008–2009?

a. demosclerosis

b. power elite theory

c. hyperpluralism

d. both a and c

23. The interest group lobbying reform of 2007 worked to

a. close loopholes in previous lobbying reform laws.

b. decrease the number of interest groups in Washington, DC.

c. allow underrepresented segments of the public to form interest groups.

d. all of the above

24. What is an issue network?

a. A shifting alliance of public and private interest groups, lawmakers, and other stakeholders focused on the same policy area.

b. The cozy relationship in one issue area between interest group lobbyist, congressional staffer, and executive branch agency.

c. An organization run by the White House staff.

d. The relationship between the president and the cabinet.

25. What are public officials' attempts in one part of the government to influence their counterparts elsewhere—in another branch or at a different (state or local) government level?

    a. judicial precedent

    b. reverse lobbying

    c. intergovernmental lobbying

    d. bureaucratic rule-making

26. Which term refers to attempts by government officials to influence interest groups on behalf of their preferred policies?

    a. reverse lobbying

    b. bureaucratic rule-making

    c. judicial precedent

    d. intergovernmental lobbying

Discussion questions

1. Discuss how sometimes disparate interest groups come together on the same side of an issue. For example, the Christian Coalition and the American Civil Liberties Union both lobby against campaign finance reform.

2. What are coalition lobbying and reverse lobbying?

3. Compare and contrast pluralism with power elite theory. Which has broader explanatory capacity?

4. Discuss the pros and cons of two-party dominance, noting the value of automatic majorities and the lack of representation that occurs.

5. Discuss the emotional attachment many people feel toward their preferred political party.

Ask them to think critically about the possible irrationality of solid partisan positions.

6. Discuss the different electoral preferences of members of the "party in the electorate" and members of "party organizations."

Video Resources

AP US Gov - Political Parties and Their Platforms www.youtube.com/watch?v=LA8aIwEwiP4

Political Parties | Crash Course Government and Politics www.pbs-learningmedia.org/resource/political-parties-crashcourse-video-1040/political-parties-crash-course-government-and-politics-40/

WatchKnowLearn.org on third parties (and the lack thereof) in the United States http://www.watchknowlearn.org/Video.aspx?VideoID=1 4226&CategoryID=3450

The Difference between Political Parties and Interest Groups https://www.youtube.com/watch?v=MOOF8p3Q11E

Website Resources

The Association for Education in Journalism and Mass Communications http://www.aejmc.org/home/about/groups/interest-groups/

The North Carolina Central University James E. Shepard Memorial Library http://shepard.libguides.nccu.edu/content.php?pid= 156096&sid=1330246

The Library of Congress http://www.loc.gov/rr/main/alcove9/usgov/intgroups.html

About.com, "US Government Info" http://usgovinfo.about.com/blorgs.htm

Shmoop.com http://www.shmoop.com/political-parties/websites.html

Ron Gunzburger's Politics http://www.politics1.com/parties.htm

Democratic National Committee http://www.democrats.org/

Republican National Committee http://www.gop.com

Libertarian Party http://www.lp.org/

Green Party http://www.gp.org/index.php

CHAPTER 14

Media and Political Communications

1. _____ is all the ways people get information about politics and the wider world.

   a. Twitter

   b. Tumblr

   c. Media

   d. World Wide Web

2. A significant change in media over the past fifty years is

   a. information comes slower

   b. more formats

   c. the public is less active in new media platforms

   d. new media outlets are less popular than the traditional ones

3. Facebook is an example of

   a. newspaper

   b. magazine

   c. old media

   d. new media

4. A role of media in a democratic system is

    a. public watchdog

    b. electing candidates

    c. broadcasting the political agenda

    d. sharing candidate ideology

5. Media can help make informed voters through the role of

    a. public watchdog

    b. providing information

    c. shaping the political agenda

    d. showing candidate mistakes

6. In the 1830s, _____ became the first mass media.

    a. letters

    b. radio

    c. telegrams

    d. newspapers

7. What is the definition of mass media?

    a. Facebook for all.

    b. Internet access for all.

    c. Media for you and me.

    d. Information and entertainment for audiences

8. Which war was known as the first media war?

    a. Korean War

    b. Spanish-American War

    c. World War I

    d. Vietnam War

9. People with strong opinions are affected by new information in what way?

   a. they change their opinion

   b. they look for similar information

   c. new information reinforces their existing opinions

   d. they ignore it

10. Between 2000 and 2015, American newspapers slashed what percentage of their staff?

    a. 40

    b. 13

    c. 3

    d. 47

11. During the 1930s, who delivered a weekly radio address known as the "Fireside Chat"?

    a. Theodore Roosevelt

    b. Karl Marx

    c. Walt Whitman

    d. Franklin Roosevelt

12. What is the primary demographic for talk radio?

    a. middle-aged white male and conservative

    b. middle-aged African American and liberal

    c. age forty-five to sixty-four white female and conservative

    d. age forty-five to sixty-four Hispanic male and liberal

13. The corporate setting helps blur the line between news, politics, and entertainment, a phenomenon now described as

    a. minor media.

    b. global information.

    c. infotainment.

    d. entertainment.

14. In new media, who chooses the material to be seen?

    a. Newspaper editor

    b. Director

    c. Producer

    d. Reader

15. How long does it take a reader to respond to a story on digital media?

    a. immediately

    b. 24 hours

    c. 48 hours

    d. 3-4 days

16. Who does the reporting for new media?

    a. Readers

    b. Traditional organization reporters

    c. Web-based reporters

    d. Editors

17. Which of the following is not considered "new media"?

    a. Facebook

    b. Twitter

    c. Internet

    d. cable news

18. What type of story attracts young viewers?

    a. sensational

b. educational

c. local interest

d. Routine

19. One of the ways the Internet could enhance democracy is by

   a. making everyone a potential news reporter.

   b. raising the bar for entry into politics.

   c. exposing fallacious points of view.

   d. allowing more people to stay at home with no need to attend public rallies.

20. Which media form is likely to include a variety of viewpoints?

   a. Facebook page

   b. Newspaper

   c. Personal Twitter

   d. Instagram

21. An example of perceived fake news is

   a. report on the number of injuries in an auto accident

   b. Global Warming is not a scientific fact

   c. Dow Jones went down 40 points

   d. The president is visiting China

22. An example of a citizen turned into a news provider is

   a. Citizen interviewed for the news

   b. Television cameraman catching an auto accident on tape

   c. Passerby filming an accident on a cellphone

   d. President answer questions at a press conference

23. Which type of media bias is most evident to academics?

    a. commercial

    b. liberal

    c. conservative

    d. realism

24. Which group is most likely to claim the media is biased?

    a. liberals

    b. Republicans

    c. Democrats

    d. the public as a whole

25. Which of the following is a media reporter likely to identify as?

    a. Republican

    b. Libertarian

    c. Democrat

    d. Independent

Discussion Questions

1. What are the pros and cons of public ownership of the media?

2. Do partisan newspapers or television stations prompt a more effective or less effective political discourse?

3. How is technology breaking down the ability of authoritarian governments to censor information?

4. What problems are caused by the "Americanization" of media around the world?

5. What possible media biases come about as the result of the profit motive?

6. How can "new media" enhance or hamper the quality of political discourse?

7. How have new technologies altered the nature and quality of news reporting; historically and today?

8. What are the pros and cons of a "Fairness Doctrine" approach to media regulation?

Video Resources

New Media and Political Communication www.youtube.com/watch?v=y6l5QGuHqOY

What's Next for Journalism and Political Communication? www.youtube.com/watch?v=b0kgR1MezGA&t=31s

Do Facts Still Matter? Media and Politics in a Post-Truth Era www.asc.upenn.edu/news-events/annenberg-video/annenberg-lecture-videos-faculty-videos/do-facts-still-matter-media-and

Saving American Journalism (NOW on PBS, 2010).

Jihad TV: Terrorism and Mass Media (2006).

State of the Union: Politics in Red and Blue (2006).

Website Resources

The Association for Education in Journalism and Mass Communications http://www.aejmc.org/home/about/groups/interest-groups/

Fact Check http://www.factcheck.org/

Center for Digital Democracy http://www.democraticmedia.org/

Fairness & Accuracy in Reporting (FAIR) http://www.fair.org/

Politifact.com's Truth-O-Meter® http://www.politifact.com/truth-o-meter/

FAIR: Challenging Media Bias Since 1986 https://fair.org/

Asia-Pacific Institute for Broadcasting Development http://www.aibd.org.my/node/1227

Mashable Social Media http://www.mashable.com/2012/04/18/social-media-and-the-news/

CHAPTER 15

Domestic Policy

1. Public policy can be defined as _____.

   a. a government plan of action to solve a social problem

   b. a ruling made by the Supreme Court that addresses a social problem

   c. an agreement among the president, Congress, and the Supreme Court to take a certain course of action

   d. a government plan of action passed only by legislatures

2. Someone who would be in favor of a policy that would provide healthcare for everyone regardless of employment status would MOST likely identify as _____.

   a. a Republican

   b. a Libertarian

   c. a Democrat

   d. a Federalist

3. Redistributive policies are relatively rare because _____.

   a. the United States is not a socialist country

   b. there is little need for them

   c. those who are the beneficiaries do not want them

    d. those who must pay for them are much better equipped to fight political battles than are potential beneficiaries

4. What is the president's role in making public policy?

    a. to create new laws based on constituent and interest group preferences

    b. to put an issue on the public agenda or include it in the budget proposal

    c. to lobby for certain bills to be passed

    d. to rule on what the government can or cannot do

5. Why are distributive policies popular?

    a. The costs are spread across taxpayers, but targeted groups receive them.

    b. The costs are generally low.

    c. The projects supported by such spending are rarely of questionable value.

    d. They often benefit the needy.

6. Which group is most likely to benefit from a distributive policy?

    a. veterans

    b. all Americans

    c. the wealthy

    d. foreign countries

7. Which is an example of a distributive policy?

    a. welfare

    b. emissions regulations

    c. a law restricting the use of the death penalty

    d. farm subsidies

8. Which statement regarding the formation of public policy is accurate?

   a. The role of Congress in making policy is relatively small compared to the role of the president.

   b. The Supreme Court holds most of the power when it comes to proposing and making policy.

   c. Solutions to public problems often generate new problems.

   d. National policies can be best thought of as packages made by Congress alone.

9. Which type of policy limits and controls the actions of individuals or groups?

   a. regulatory

   b. redistributive

   c. foreign

   d. distributive

10. _____ is the second step in making policy.

   a. Policy evaluation

   b. Policy formulation

   c. Policy implementation

   d. Policy adoption

11. Government agencies have their largest role in _____.

   a. agenda setting

   b. policy adoption

   c. policy implementation

   d. policy formulation

12. Policies that are aimed at improving the quality of life for those in need are known generally as _____.

    a. lending-hand policies

    b. group-effort policies

    c. distributive policies

    d. social policies

13. Anita participates in a government program that requires her to submit a pay stub and other documents in order to receive income assistance. This is an example of _____.

    a. a distributive program

    b. a means-tested program

    c. a social insurance program

    d. a public policy

14. Public policy that seeks to meet the basic needs of people who are unable to provide for themselves is _____ policy.

    a. civil rights

    b. social welfare

    c. regulatory

    d. distributive

15. What was the primary purpose of the Aid to Families with Dependent Children program?

    a. to make sure poor families could support their children

    b. to make sure children could eat school lunch

    c. to make sure families with more than one child could afford basic needs

    d. to make sure single mothers could care for their children

16. What are social insurance policies?

    a. programs funded by only one group of taxpayers that are distributed only to noncitizens

    b. programs that protect people from losing their homes during a natural disaster

    c. government programs that offer benefits in exchange for contributions

    d. programs designed to restrict or change the behavior of certain groups or individuals

17. Most social welfare policies can be categorized as _____.

    a. entitlement programs

    b. regulatory policies

    c. private policies

    d. redistributive policies

18. Which is a way the Social Security trust fund could be made sustainable?

    a. lowering the retirement age

    b. increasing taxes

    c. increasing benefit levels

    d. eliminating means-testing

19. A federal program that guarantees benefits to all qualified recipients is known as _____.

    a. a welfare program

    b. a mandate program

    c. a means-tested program

    d. an entitlement program

20. Financial incentives given by the government to corporations, individuals, or other governments for the purpose of encouraging certain activities or behaviors are _____.

    a. entitlements

    b. subsidies

    c. welfare programs

    d. grants

21. How did the Great Depression impact American public policy?

    a. The government realized that it had to eliminate environmental restrictions on businesses to help them prosper, which set back efforts to pass stronger environmental policies.

    b. It was the first time that education subsidies were provided to the middle class.

    c. For the first time, people began to view poverty as a problem requiring government action.

    d. The government put more pressure on churches and businesses to help eradicate poverty.

22. Which was a major criticism of the Aid to Families with Dependent Children (AFDC) program?

    a. It had no work requirements.

    b. Families were able to receive aid only for a short period of time.

    c. The aid to most families was not sufficient to meet basic needs.

    d. Too many poor people received no aid.

23. _____ is a welfare program of block grants to states that encourages recipients to work in exchange for time-limited benefits

    a. Aid to Families with Dependent Children

    b. Temporary Assistance to Needy Families

c. Supplemental Nutrition Assistance Program

d. Social Security

24. _____ is an example of a social insurance program.

a. Aid to Families with Dependent Children

b. Temporary Assistance to Needy Families

c. Medicare

d. Supplemental Nutrition Assistance Program

25. Prior to the health care reform that was passed in 2010, the government's role in health care was limited to _____.

a. Medicare and Medicaid

b. Temporary Assistance to Needy Families

c. United State Universal Healthcare

d. the Patient Protection Act

26. The federal government's insurance program for the elderly and disabled is called _____.

a. AFDC

b. Medicaid

c. Medicare

d. AARP

27. Which is likely the strongest ideological argument against a system of universal health care in the United States?

a. Such a system has not been adopted in an industrialized country like the United States.

b. The American public is generally satisfied with the current system.

c. The costs of Medicare and Medicaid would skyrocket under such a system.

d. A universal health care policy runs against the American economic system and gives the government too much control.

28. What type of policy addresses the problem of economic security for society as a whole?

   a. social welfare

   b. economic

   c. private

   d. social insurance

29. The basic principles that regulate the economic market and influence the price of a good are known as laws of _____.

   a. antitrust policy

   b. supply and demand

   c. production and consumption

   d. monetary policy

30. Fiscal policy refers to _____.

   a. the government's use of taxing and spending powers to regulate the economy

   b. the use of interest rates to control the money supply in order to regulate the economy

   c. policies designed to regulate business, labor, and trade

   d. regulations designed to regulate business, labor, and trade

31. The manipulation of interest rates to control the money supply in order to regulate the economy is known as _____ policy.

   a. budgetary

   b. monetary

   c. fiscal

   d. regulatory

32. Monetary policy is _____ policy.

    a. a distributive

    b. a redistributive

    c. a regulatory

    d. a fiscal

33. A tax levied on returns from capital investments, such as profits from the sale of real estate, is _____ tax.

    a. a capital gains

    b. an excise

    c. a consumption

    d. a value-added

34. The policy that says the United States should put its interest first and not interfere in global concerns is known as _____.

    a. the Reagan Doctrine

    b. manifest destiny

    c. "One Hemisphere"

    d. isolationism

35. Which is an example of an intergovernmental organization?

    a. the United Nations

    b. Greenpeace

    c. the U.S. State Department

    d. General Motors

36. Foreign policy that lays out a country's basic stance toward international actors or issues is _____.

    a. foreign economic policy

    b. structural defense policy

    c. crisis policy

    d. strategic policy

37. The Cold War policy of the United States seeking to prevent the spread of communism is an example of _____.

    a. isolationism

    b. roll-back

    c. containment

    d. the domino theory

38. The State Department is the executive department responsible for managing _____.

    a. military affairs

    b. foreign affairs

    c. Medicaid and Medicare

    d. parks and forests

39. The Department of Defense is responsible for _____.

    a. manufacturing expensive and secret weapons

    b. managing the country's military personnel, equipment, and operations

    c. conducting espionage

    d. advising the president on how to execute his powers as commander-in-chief

40. The _____ was Congress's attempt to limit the president's ability to use troops in hostilities without congressional approval

    a. War Powers Act

    b. Gulf of Tonkin Resolution

    c. National Defense Act

    d. Helms-Burton Act

41. True or False: Distributive policies are popular because their costs are not noticed as they are spread among all taxpayers, but their benefits go to a specific group who knows they are benefitting.

42. True or False: Government agencies have their largest role in policy evaluation.

43. True or False: Public policy that seeks to meet the basic needs of people who are unable to provide for themselves is social welfare policy.

44. True or False: A federal program that guarantees benefits to qualified recipients is an entitlement program.

45. True or False: Economic policy addresses the problem of economic security for the benefit of the wealthiest members of society.

46. True or False: Tax policy is a regulatory policy.

47. True or False: The system of 12 banks run by a board of governors with a chair who is appointed by the president is known as the Federal Reserve.

48. True or False: U.S. foreign policy is almost always carried out for the good of American citizens or in the interest of national security.

49. True or False: According to the concept of isolationism, in order for the United States to be safe, the country must be actively engaged in shaping the global environment and be willing to intervene.

50. True or False: Nike and Apple are examples of multinational corporations.

Discussion Questions

1. Class brainstorms on events from the past. How did these events change public policy? Did the changes go far enough to assist in future similar events, or is more change needed?

2. How can the United States wean itself from foreign oil?

3. How can the United States improve its trade deficit?

4. How should the United States concern itself with other nations?

Video Resources

A Civil Action (1998)

Hacking Democracy (2006) HBO Films

How Weed Won the West (2012) Sacred Cow Productions

Kansas v. Darwin (2008) Unconditional Films

PBS Frontline: "The Card Game"

Prohibition (2011) Ken Burns and Lynn Novick

Why We Fight (2005)

No End in Sight (2007) Magnolia

The Fog of War (2003) Sony Pictures Classic

Argo (2012) GK Films

United States Domestic Policy - Harvard Kennedy School http://iop.harvard.edu/forum/united-states-domestic-policy

Developing Domestic Policy www.c-span.org/video/?286994-2/developing-domestic-policy

DomesticPolicyIssueswww.c-span.org/video/?73714-1/domestic-policy-issues

US ELECTIONS AND DOMESTIC POLICY www.sipa.columbia. edu/file/us-elections-and-domestic-policy

Website Resources

Maps of War http://www.mapsofwar.com/

Foreign Policy http://www.foreignpolicy.com/

Foreign Policy Research Institute http://www.fpri.org

The White House http://www.whitehouse.gov/issues/foreign-policy

Foreign Affairs http://www.foreignaffairs.com/

The Brookings Institution www.brookings.edu/

Policy Studies Journal http://onlinelibrary.wiley.com/journal/10.1111/ (ISSN)1541-0072

Institute for Women's Policy Research www.iwpr.org/

Rand Corporation http://www.rand.org/

Urban Institute http://www.urban.org/?gclid=CKSe8eCxpLMCFcaDQ god1AUAnw

CHAPTER 16

Foreign Policy

1. What does United States foreign policy determine?

    a. how the United States government filters who is eligible or not for the redistribution of wealth, often utilizing means-tested programs.

    b. how the United States government coordinates federal transportation projects to enhance national economic competitiveness.

    c. how the United States government reacts and responds to governments and non-governmental groups well beyond its borders.

    d. how the United States government develops longer-term distributive programs that provide benefits to a specific segment of the population.

2. Why is foreign policy one of the most critical to United States' national security?

    a. America's security as a rich, stable and peaceful country may come under threat without an adequate foreign policy.

    b. The current global order is based on the maintenance of alliances.

    c. America cannot act alone to pursue its own interests.

    d. The search of new markets for American companies.

3. What are isolationists' viewpoints regarding to foreign policy?

   a. Interventionism is acceptable but only up to a certain degree.

   b. America should intervene in the affairs of other countries but avoid going to war at any cost.

   c. America should focus on itself and not intervene in the affairs of other countries.

   d. America should indirectly intervene in the affairs of other countries by third-party actors.

4. Why do some experts perceive that isolationism has been a failure in the United States?

   a. Because of the poor experience after World War II. Results were not as satisfactory as expected.

   b. Because interventionism has been more effective than isolationism to benefit the interests of the American people.

   c. Because Latin America is very unstable, and thus, poses a risk to the United States.

   d. Because isolationism means less profit and work for the defence industry.

5. What is interventionists' main viewpoint regarding to foreign policy?

   a. Interventionism is necessary for the liberal global order based on democracy, free-trade, and Western international institutions.

   b. Interventionism is sometimes needed to restore law and order in foreign countries.

   c. Interventionism can help in creating a stable environment for transitioning states.

   d. To keep the republic safe, America should be actively engaged in shaping the global political order and willing to do what it takes to create the desired outcomes.

6. What is American Exceptionalism?

   a. A concept that teaches that the United States is unique because of its notion of equality, self-rule, and limited government.

   b. A concept that teaches that the United States is unique because of its intensely antiliberal character, which is rooted in a sense of its special mission.

   c. A concept that teaches that the United States is a great global power, and uses it sparingly.

   d. None of the above.

7. What is the influence of American exceptionalism in United States foreign policy?

   a. American exceptionalism is the core of imperialist foreign policy.

   b. Policymakers perceive that America has a special mission to spread the benefits of its particular liberal political system globally.

   c. The United States is divinely destined to rule the world.

   d. None of the above.

8. True or False: International bodies, such as the United Nations, NATO, and OPEC, work together to create agreements among nations regarding international policies.

9. True or False: The Department of Defense (DOD) manages the United States military and its equipment to protect the nation.

10. Which of these is defined as the president's inner circle that advises on matters of foreign policy and is coordinated by the national security adviser?

    a. The White House.

    b. Department of State.

    c. Department of Defense.

    d. National Security Council.

11. Which is the biggest government's agency in the United States?

    a. Department of Defense.

    b. Department of State.

    c. CIA.

    d. None of the above.

12. Which executive department is charged with managing foreign affairs?

    a. Department of State.

    b. Department of Interior.

    c. Department of Justice.

    d. Department of Treasury.

13. Which executive department is charged with helping the economy expand through working to ensure fair trade?

    a. Department of State.

    b. Department of Interior.

    c. Department of Commerce.

    d. Department of Treasury.

14. True or False: U.S. foreign policy is related to the country's trade policy objectives since in recent decades they have included reducing protections both at home and abroad.

15. Who is responsible for developing and recommending trade policy to the U.S. president?

    a. Secretary of State.

    b. United States Trade Representative.

    c. Secretary of Commerce.

    d. Secretary of Treasury.

16. The United States has been a member of the WTO since

    a. 1945

    b. 1933

    c. 2001

    d. 1995

17. True or False: Tariffs are actually a type of tax paid on goods sourced from other countries and usually paid to United States customs authorities by importing companies.

18. True or False: the Joint Chiefs of Staff act as service chiefs of the Army, Navy, Marine Corps, Air Force, Space Force, and the National Guard Bureau.

19. How many service members and civilians does the Department of Defense employ?

    a. Almost 2 million

    b. Almost 3 million

    c. 1 million

    d. Almost 5 million

20. True or False: American liberal internationalists argue that America needs the transatlantic relationship because it lends legitimacy to its global leadership

21. True or False: Russia opposes proposals for Ukrainian membership of NATO because Russians fear the spread of United States influence in Eastern Europe.

22. Which of these is a source of contemporary American exceptionalism?

    a. Military primacy

    b. Economic dynamism

c. Political diversity

d. All of the above

23. True or False: Cultural homogeneity is a source of contemporary American exceptionalism

24. Why might American exceptionalism likely lead to opposition to a central world government?

a. Its general anti-statism

b. Its individualistic core

c. Its fascist core

d. All of the above

25. True or False: The U.S. acting president can initiate war without prior express military authorization from Congress.

26. How many times in history have U.S. presidents initiated war without prior express military authorization from Congress?

a. On at least 100 occasions

b. On at least 200 occasions

c. On at least 35 occasions

D. On at least 125 occasions

Discussion questions

1. What are the advantages and disadvantages of an isolationist foreign policy?

2. What are the advantages and disadvantages of an interventionist foreign policy?

3. In what ways foreign policy might be more challenging than domestic policy?

4. What do you know about the U.S. Department of State?

5. Why does the United States offer foreign assistance to other countries?

6. What is the Universal Declaration of Human Rights?

7. How does diplomacy help promote trade, commerce, and investment?

8. How did the collapse of the Soviet Union affect U.S. foreign policy? Is it now more complex or simpler?

9. Should the United States maintain the NATO alliance, even if doing so will likely create more conflicts with Russia?

Video resources

The US' Overseas Military Base Strategy www.youtube.com/watch?v=A0qt0hdCQtg

Media Education Foundation http://www.mediaed.org/

Icount https://icount.com/

PBS Frontline http://www.pbs.org/wgbh/pages/frontline/view/

The United States and NATO www.nato.int/cps/en/natohq/declassified_162350.htm

Navigating US-Russia relations in 2020 and beyond www.brookings.edu/blog/order-from-chaos/2020/01/09/highlights-navigating-us-russia-r

A New Vision for American Foreign Policy https://www.youtube.com/watch?v=KsQYkvDB9L4

Early 1800s US Foreign Policy https://billofrightsinstitute.org/videos/early-1800s-us-foreign-policy-homework-help

Iceland and NATO https://www.nato.int/cps/en/natohq/declassified_162083.htm

Website Resources

Real Clear Politics http://www.realclearpolitics.com/welcomead/?ref= http://www.realclearpolitics.com/

International Affairs http://www.internationalaffairs.com/

United Nations http://www.un.org/

Maps of War http://www.mapsofwar.com/

Foreign Policy http://www.foreignpolicy.com/

Foreign Policy Research Institute http://www.fpri.org

The White House http://www.whitehouse.gov/issues/foreign-policy

Foreign Affairs http://www.foreignaffairs.com/

The Brookings Institution www.brookings.edu/

Policy Studies Journal http://onlinelibrary.wiley.com/journal/10.1111/ (ISSN)1541-0072

FirstGov http://www.firstgov.gov/

US Agency For International Development http://www.usaid.gov/

Factbook-CIAWorldFactbookhttps://www.cia.gov/library/publications/ the-world-factbook/

Answer Key

Chapter 1	Chapter 2	Chapter 3	Chapter 4
Question 1: A	Question 1: T	Question 1: D	Question 1: B
Question 2: B	Question 2: D	Question 2: B	Question 2: A
Question 3: B	Question 3: B	Question 3: D	Question 3: A
Question 4: D	Question 4: A	Question 4: B	Question 4: D
Question 5: B	Question 5: A	Question 5: D	Question 5: B
Question 6: C	Question 6: B	Question 6: A	Question 6: A
Question 7: A	Question 7: B	Question 7: B	Question 7: B
Question 8: A	Question 8: T	Question 8: B	Question 8: A
Question 9: D	Question 9: T	Question 9: A	Question 9: B
Question 10: A	Question 10: F	Question 10: D	Question 10: A
Question 11: C	Question 11: A	Question 11: B	Question 11: A
Question 12: C	Question 12: F	Question 12: D	Question 12: A
Question 13: B	Question 13: C	Question 13: C	Question 13: B
Question 14: B	Question 14: C	Question 14: D	Question 14: C
Question 15: C	Question 15: B	Question 15: T	Question 15: A
Question 16: C	Question 16: A	Question 16: D	Question 16: B
Question 17: C	Question 17: D	Question 17: T	Question 17: B
Question 18: A	Question 18: B	Question 18: F	Question 18: B
Question 19: C	Question 19: T	Question 19: F	Question 19: D
Question 20: B	Question 20: F	Question 20: T	Question 20: A
Question 21: T	Question 21: B	Question 21: F	Question 21: A
Question 22: A	Question 22: T	Question 22: T	Question 22: C
Question 23: D	Question 23: D	Question 23: F	Question 23: D
Question 24: F	Question 24: F	Question 24: T	Question 24: C
Question 25: T	Question 25: C	Question 25: T	Question 25: B

Question 26: B

Question 27: A

Question 28: A

Question 29: B

Question 30: D

Question 31: D

Question 32: A

Question 33: A

Question 34: B

Question 35: A

Question 36: C

Question 37: A

Question 38: C

Question 39: A

Question 40: A

Question 41: B

Question 42: A

Chapter 5:

Question 1: C

Question 2: D

Question 3: A

Question 4: D

Question 5: D

Question 6: B

Question 7: C

Question 8: C

Question 9: C

Question 10: D

Question 11: C

Question 12: C

Question 13: B

Question 14: D

Question 15: C

Question 16: A

Question 17: C

Question 18: C

Question 19: C

Question 20: C

Question 21: D

Question 22: A

Question 23: D

Question 24: B

Question 25: C

Question 26: B

Question 27: D

Question 28: C

Question 29: B

Question 30: A

Question 31: C

Question 32: A

Question 33: C

Question 34: B

Question 35: C

Question 36: D

Question 37: B

Question 38: D

Question 39: A

Question 40: C

Question 41: D

Question 42: A

Question 43: B

Question 44: B

Question 45: C

Question 46: B

Question 47: C

Question 48: D

Question 49: D

Question 50: A

Question 51: C

Chapter 6

Question 1: A

Question 2: A

Question 3: B

Question 4: B

Question 5: A

Question 6: C

Question 7: D

Question 8: A

Question 9: C

Question 10: C

Question 11: C

Question 12: A

Question 13: B

Question 14: B

Question 15: A

Question 16: B

Question 17: A

Question 18: B

Question 19: A

Question 20: A

Question 21: A

Question 22: B

Question 23: C

Question 24: A

Question 25: B

Question 26: B

Question 27: A

Question 28: A

Question 29: C

Question 30: B

Question 31: A

Question 32: D

Question 33: D

Question 34: D

Question 35: B

Question 36: C

Question 37: B

Question 38: B

Question 39: D

Question 40: A

Question 41: A

Question 42: C

Question 43: A

Question 44: D

Question 45: B

Question 46: A

Question 47: A

Question 48: B

Question 49: B

Question 50: B

Question 51: B

Question 52: A

Question 53: C

Question 54: A

Question 55: C

Question 56: A

Question 57: D

Question 58: A

Question 59: C

Question 60: A

Question 61: D

Question 62: C

Question 63: B

Question 64: B

Question 65: A

Question 66: A

Question 67: C

Question 68: C

Question 69: B

Question 70: A

Question 71: C

Question 72: C

Chapter 7:

Question 1: A

Question 2: B

Question 3: A

Question 4: B

Question 5: B

Question 6: A

Question 7: D

Question 8: B

Question 9: A

Question 10: A

Question 11: C

Question 12: C

Question 13: C

Question 14: C

Question 15: B

Question 16: C

Question 17: C

Question 18: B

Question 19: D

Question 20: A

Question 21: C

Question 22: A

Question 23: C

Question 24: B

Question 25: D

Question 26: A

Question 27: D

Question 28: B

Question 29: B

Question 30: D

Question 31: B

Question 32: C

Question 33: A

Question 34: B

Question 35: C

Question 36: D

Question 37: A

Question 38: C

Question 39: D

Question 40: C

Chapter 8:

Question 1: C

Question 2: C

Question 3: A

Question 4: B

Question 5: C

Question 6: A

Question 7: B

Question 8: B

Question 9: C

Question 10: B

Question 11: B

Question 12: B

Question 13: C

Question 14: C

Question 15: A

Question 16: B

Question 17: B

Question 18: A

Question 19: T

Question 20: F

Question 21: T

Question 22: T

Question 23: F

Question 24: F

Question 25: T

Question 26: T

Question 27: F

Question 28: T

Chapter 9:

Question 1: A

Question 2: B

Question 3: A

Question 4: C

Question 5: A

Question 6: B

Question 7: C

Question 8: A

Question 9: C

Question 10: B

Question 11: B

Question 12: B

Question 13: B

Question 14: C

Question 15: C

Question 16: B

Question 17: A

Question 18: D

Question 19: A

Question 20: B

Question 21: A

Question 22: A

Question 23: B

Question 24: A

Question 25: A

Question 26: B

Question 27: B

Question 28: A

Question 29: C

Question 30: A

Question 31: B

Question 32: B

Question 33: B

Question 34: B

Question 35: C

Chapter 10:

Question 1: B

Question 2: C

Question 3: B

Question 4: B

Question 5: C

Question 6: C

Question 7: C

Question 8: C

Question 9: D

Question 10: B

Question 11: C

Question 12: B

Question 13: C

Question 14: A

Question 15: C

Question 16: C

Question 17: B

Question 18: B

Question 19: B

Question 20: B

Question 21: C

Question 22: C

Question 23: B

Question 24: C

Question 25: B

Question 26: A

Question 27: A

Question 28: B

Question 29: C

Question 30: B

Question 31: A

Question 32: A

Question 33: D

Question 34: C

Question 35: D

Question 36: B

Question 37: A

Question 38: B

Question 39: D

Question 40: B

Question 41: B

Question 42: B

Question 43: A

Question 44: B

Question 45: D

Question 46: B

Question 47: C

Question 48: B

Question 49: C

Question 50: A

Question 51: B

Question 52: B

Question 53: C

Question 54: B

Question 55: C

Question 56: B

Question 57: A

Question 58: A

Question 59: D

Question 60: A

Question 61: B

Question 62: C

Question 63: A

Question 64: B

Question 65: C

Question 66: B

Question 67: C

Chapter 11:

Question 1: C

Question 2: A

Question 3: D

Question 4: A

Question 5: A

Question 6: A

Question 7: A

Question 8: A

Question 9: C

Question 10: B

Question 11: D

Question 12: A

Question 13: A

Question 14: D

Question 15: C

Question 16: D

Question 17: C

Question 18: A

Question 19: B

Question 20: A

Question 21: C

Question 22: A

Question 23: A

Question 24: A

Question 25: C

Question 26: A

Question 27: C

Question 28: C

Question 29: C

Question 30: C

Question 31: D

Question 32: B

Question 33: B

Question 34: B

Question 35: C

Chapter 12:

Question 1: C

Question 2: A

Question 3: D

Question 4: A

Question 5: B

Question 6: D

Question 7: A

Question 8: D

Question 9: D

Question 10: A

Question 11: D

Question 12: A

Question 13: D

Question 14: A

Question 15: D

Question 16: A

Question 17: B

Question 18: C

Question 19: C

Question 20: F

Question 21: F

Question 22: C

Question 23: T

Question 24: B

Question 25: T

Chapter 13:

Question 1: C

Question 2: B

Question 3: A

Question 4: D

Question 5: B

Question 6: A

Question 7: D

Question 8: B

Question 9: A

Question 10: D

Question 11: D

Question 12: B

Question 13: A

Question 14: A

Question 15: B

Question 16: A

Question 17: A

Question 18: D

Question 19: D

Question 20: D

Question 21: A

Question 22: B

Question 23: A

Question 24: A

Question 25: C

Question 26: A

Chapter 14:

Question 1: C

Question 2: B

Question 3: D

Question 4: A

Question 5: B

Question 6: D

Question 7: D

Question 8: B

Question 9: C

Question 10: A

Question 11: D

Question 12: A

Question 13: C

Question 14: D

Question 15: A

Question 16: B

Question 17: D

Question 18: A

Question 19: A

Question 20: B

Question 21: B

Question 22: C

Question 23: A

Question 24: B

Question 25: D

Chapter 15:

Question 1: A

Question 2: C

Question 3: D

Question 4: B

Question 5: A

Question 6: A

Question 7: D

Question 8: C

Question 9: A

Question 10: B

Question 11: C

Question 12: D

Question 13: B

Question 14: B

Question 15: A

Question 16: C

Question 17: D

Question 18: B

Question 19: D

Question 20: B

Question 21: C

Question 22: A

Question 23: B

Question 24: C

Question 25: A

Question 26: C

Question 27: D

Question 28: B

Question 29: B

Question 30: A

Question 31: B

Question 32: C

Question 33: A

Question 34: D

Question 35: A

Question 36: D

Question 37: C

Question 38: B

Question 39: B

Question 40: A

Question 41: T

Question 42: F

Question 43: T

Question 44: T

Question 45: F

Question 46: F

Question 47: T

Question 48: T

Question 49: F

Question 50: T

Chapter 16:

Question 1: C

Question 2: A

Question 3: C

Question 4: A

Question 5: D

Question 6: A

Question 7: B

Question 8: T

Question 9: T

Question 10: D

Question 11: A

Question 12: A

Question 13: C

Question 14: T

Question 15: B

Question 16: D

Question 17: T

Question 18: T

Question 19: B

Question 20: T

Question 21: T

Question 22: D

Question 23: F

Question 24: A

Question 25: T

Question 26: D

About the Author

R. L. Cohen is a university lecturer residing in Redlands, California. His research focus is on political science, ethics, and religious studies. When he is not lecturing, he often can be found at the beach, at a unique coffee bar, or traveling back to his home in New Zealand.

Printed in the USA
CPSIA information can be obtained
at www.ICGtesting.com
LVHW010011250923
759176LV00046B/999